THE ST OF DREAMS

Fantasy, Anxiety and Psychoanalysis

Kirsty Hall

KARNAC

First published in 2007 by
Karnac Books Ltd.
118 Finchley Road
London NW3 5HT

British Library Cataloguing in Publication Data
A C.I.P. for this book is available from the British Library

ISBN-13: 978-1-85575-496-6

Edited, designed, and produced by Florence Production Ltd,
www.florenceproduction.co.uk

Printed in Great Britain

www.karnacbooks.com

THE STUFF OF DREAMS

For Chris, Duncan and Martin

CONTENTS

ACKNOWLEDGEMENTS

T he ideas that form the core of this book started out in a rather different guise. I thought I might write something about the problematic distinction between training and education. Fantasies and anxieties intervened, and --at an early stage of writing it gradually became clear that this is a project of a very different kind—an exploration of the curious relationship between fantasy on the one hand and anxiety on the other. In fact of course, they cannot really be so simply separated, since one often engenders and/or temporarily dispels or displaces the other. The process of writing has largely been a part of my education rather than a training exercise since, in my view, fantasies play a large part in education and have only a minor place in training. Writing itself is often an act of fantasising in the face of anxiety.

I owe a debt to many people. I wish to thank Pat Elliot for her careful reading and comments on many of the chapters in the book, often at an early stage of drafting and for keeping me up to date with the change of the seasons in Canada. Susan Budd encouraged me to read more widely for the chapter on religion in the course of our stimulating walks on Hampstead Heath. Philip Derbyshire pointed out that my analysis of anxiety needed reworking. My colleagues during my time at Middlesex University, Bernard Burgoyne, Alan Rowan, Julia Borossa and Lucia Corti patiently listened to my account of the book's progress at many stages and offered at various times, advice, information, critical dissection of some of its key themes and support throughout. Carla Lathe and her husband Anthony sharpened up the introduction. Students and members of the Site for Contemporary Psychoanalysis and the Guild of Psychotherapists have heard about parts of this book as work in progress and provided welcome comments and criticism.

Finally, my family have patiently read and commented on chapters of the book over the years and put up with the well-worn phrase, "it's nearly finished". Now it is. The errors, omissions and opinions expressed in this book are all my responsibility.

Extracts from the following work is reprinted with permission:

Quotations from Kinks, *Dedicated Follower of Fashion*, The Sanctuary Group plc. *DEDICATED FOLLOWER OF FASHION – Words and Music by Ray Davies – © 1966 Davray Music Ltd and Carlin Music Corp London NW1 8BD – All Rights Reserved – Used by Permission.*

Kirsty Hall
October 2006

Introduction

Bliss was it in that dawn to be alive,
But to be young was very heaven!
(Wordsworth, *The Prelude. Book* xi, 1805)

Today, belief in revolutions has gone out of fashion and the truth of Wordsworth's famous quotation, set in the context of the French Revolution, is in doubt. We no longer believe in utopian futures, but on the other hand—perhaps as rather poor compensation—gothic fantasy and science fiction now have a huge following.

At least one person in six in countries such as Britain or the United States will be diagnosed with a mental illness at some time in their lives; some studies suggest figures as high as one in four. These figures include people suffering a vast range of crippling experiences —depression, anorexia, phobia, panic attacks and the like.

Many people would regard the contents of those two paragraphs as being topics for entirely separate discussion using different criteria for evaluation and judgement of the issues they pose. This book proposes that, in fact, there are complex, often unnoticed links between fantasies of all kinds and anxieties, both in the public sphere and in the inner reaches of the individual mind. Making a connection between them offers the opportunity of bringing together several fields of enquiry. However, this book does not set out to produce a comprehensive overarching theory of fantasy and anxiety;

1

it hopes to entertain, to intrigue the reader and to leave her or him with few if any answers, but rather, a new range of questions. To this end, popular cultural references to anxiety and fantasy, such as *Fahrenheit 9–11* and *The Simpsons*, will be used to illustrate and enliven the discussion.

Some chapters have a short illustration drawn from practical situations often found in the consulting rooms of analysts, therapists and counsellors, but not based on any individual patient. In this field, writers often offer copious clinical material to illustrate a single theoretical proposition. I have attempted to write this book starting from the opposite point of view. Thus the aim is to present a series of interlinked theoretical arguments with a few illustrations to bring the ideas to life and weave the arguments together. The book may incidentally provide helpful hints to practitioners but the clinical references are really intended for everyone, to put clothes on the bones of occasionally complex abstract arguments. The book raises philosophical as well as practical questions about the nature of both anxiety and fantasy.

Fantasy is at the heart of this book and the fantasies discussed are not simply those heard in the consulting room. For these reasons, other chapters use quotations from a wide range of literature to provide a key illustrative theme. Here is a straightforward example. In Thurber's short story, "The Secret Life of Walter Mitty", Mitty is a henpecked husband constantly escaping from the never-ending demands of his wife. Whilst parking the car to collect the dry-cleaning, he savours a daydream that he is a surgeon about to save a patient's life by improvising with his fountain-pen before "coreopsis" sets in. He is interrupted by an attendant pointing out that he is entering the car park via the lane marked "Exit Only". (Thurber, 1945, pp. 70–1) Indeed, many of the best moments in life can be those "Mittyesque" moments where we are not "doing" anything—staring out of the window admiring a view or imagining ourselves as the heroic central figure in a dramatic scenario.

This book explains why fantasies, daydreaming, comedy and jokes are not just accidental by-products of living. They can make life fun, spicing up the boring moments. Even if they are sometimes completely pointless, at other times fantasies perform an often essential task, that of making the experience of being human bearable. Perhaps more than ever before, fantasies of all kinds need protection from the outside world. Our dreams need to be preserved, kept intact and defended. Our private inner worlds are what allow each of us to be unique, individual and most importantly, to experience, if we are lucky, some joy, meaning and happiness in our lives. If we are less fortunate, then our fantasies and dreams can haunt us turning into nightmares and gothic horror.

How do fantasies work? What is their purpose in life? We are surrounded by them in the form of Star Trek, gothic fiction, soaps of every kind as well the more traditional forms of the classical symphony and the novel. Once humans acquired speech, they didn't simply use it for obviously practical purposes like telling everyone else where the best sources of food were: they told each other stories. Why?

When we are not awake and searching for food, procreating, working, arguing with each other and so forth, we spend a about of third of our lives asleep, apparently uselessly—allowing sleep researchers the pleasure of spending much of their time trying to work out why this should be so. It is curious that there seems to be no similar degree of interest in that other common quasi-unconscious condition, daydreaming. I have never seen daydreaming featured as such in a checklist of tasks to be carried out in completing a project—yet, in management speak, it does have a respectable and recognised first cousin: the brainstorming session. Here, immediate thoughts, often including wild and wacky ideas, are thrown out by the group at random; only later are these ideas whittled down, organised and refined into a coherent plan. Essentially, participants are allowed and indeed encouraged to think of new ideas without the restraint of practical considerations or what people might think of as being "acceptable". In "real life"—just possibly—Walter Mitty's idea of using a fountain-pen in his fantasised operation on his "patient" might work temporarily, since it is the kind of thought that would lead one to improvise in an emergency. However, another aspect of his fantasies is clearly impossible. "Coreopsis" cannot "set in"—it is the name of a flower belonging to the aster family!

When daydreaming and the wilder fantasies of a brainstorming session enter the domain of public ideas, they become the stuff of fantasy, a genre that is all around us. Popular fiction aimed apparently at children but read just as avidly by adults is at the top of bestseller lists in the guise of J.K. Rowling and Philip Pullman.

Science fiction such as *Star Trek* appears nightly on the television and our film screens and we should of course add the gothic genre whether it is *Dracula* or *Buffy the Vampire Slayer*.

So how much of our lives do we spend fantasying? A teasing answer might be: "as long as a piece of string"—our fantasies can be tailored to fit our personal whim. The opposite, or more precisely, opposing, experience is the increasing insistence in the contemporary world on the bureaucracy surrounding us—drives toward transparency, accountability, efficiency and precise deadlines. These are all anathema to fantasy. Perhaps it is partly a question of trust. Onora O'Neill devoted the Reith lectures in 2002 to the fact that deadlines, targets and quality assurance increasingly fill the working lives of those of us who are foolish enough to imagine we are paid to think or even to fantasise about what might be, rather than simply consider what already is (O'Neill, 2002). We are often made to feel that too long spent daydreaming gets nothing worthwhile done. What is much more rarely recognised is that no time spent daydreaming can lead us down the path of boredom and bleak depression.

The language of fantasy is derided: "it doesn't matter really"; "it's just an idle thought"; "it's a silly idea" or "it's only a dream" are everyday examples. More extended manifestations of fantasy such as doodles and jokes (whether good or bad) are similarly regarded as trivia. Impossible scenarios such as spending the next six months alone on a Scottish island writing a book without a single interruption from the family, the patients, the university, the mobile phone, and the email inbox, to mention the first distractions that come to mind, are treated dismissively. Yet their public equivalents—art, cinema, soaps, situation comedy, fantasy thrillers, bonkbusters and the like—reflect the fact that, in another mode, we all need and value such idleness when it is allowed to flourish and develop into something many of us enjoy.

Fantasy is locked in a battle for survival in a world dominated by desires of the great and the good for transparency, accountability, bureaucracy and the achievement of goals. This dichotomy is evident even in classical writing. The poems of Ovid remain startlingly contemporary and a lyrically described love tryst on a hot summer afternoon is somehow much more attractive than Caesar's plodding account of his conquest of Gaul written in the style of a model examination answer. Yet, the bureaucrats would have us learn "useful" lessons from history rather than have our imaginations fired by a poet who died more than two thousand years ago.

Fantasy and daydreaming are not just a means of avoiding the dead hand of bureaucracy. As I have indicated, in their "readymade" forms they exist as science fiction, fantasy novels, gothic films, computer games, TV and so on; in our heads we have a private world of imagining including dreams, nightmares, speculations, sexual scenarios and so forth. Fantasies have a purpose and we need them —they keep our anxieties from overwhelming us. It may seem paradoxical, but preoccupation with carrying out the imperatives of the checklist and the demands of the working day, whilst often experienced very differently, achieve the same object through different means—they also keep our anxieties from overwhelming us. Caesar's conquest of Gaul is indeed a useful account for historians. How well it may have served him personally as a way of keeping his own private and possibly disturbing thoughts at bay, we shall never know. Writing in a literal sense (and style) keeps one's thoughts tidily organised. Poetry is at the other end of a continuum— it allows fantasy its head, expanding the quality of experience but also allowing effects to be created beyond the words themselves. Indeed the world of fantasy is by no means simply pleasurable. The attachment of people to their private fantasies is often full of ambiguity. For every Walter Mitty style fantasy, there is someone else experiencing painful and loathsome fantasies in form of nightmares and flashbacks of scenes of killing, torture and abuse. What is the relationship if any between the pleasure and pain of such varied experiences?

* * *

Anxiety is just as chimerical as fantasy. It takes many forms: stress of myriad kinds, fear of death, fear of living, fear of relationships, fear of flying, fear of spiders—the list is just as endless as the list of people's fantasies. Like fantasy, however, anxiety has what is, at first sight, a very puzzling property—we both love and loathe it. If most of us were completely satisfied with or utterly terrified of our lives as they are, then why do the majority of us, nevertheless, get out of bed in the morning? Perhaps the answer lies in the fact that human beings have complex patterns of thinking that, in the main, do not lie at extreme ends of the emotional spectrum. Why is happiness connected to more than just snuggling under the duvet congratulating ourselves on our good fortune in being alive? Equally however, if we are really and truly terrified of the world we live in and everything connected with it, then why don't we cower underneath the same duvet and refuse to come out to face another difficult and frightening day? If we have the good fortune to be currently reasonably prosperous and not too emotionally stressed, in the "real" world, we eventually get up because hunger beckons and/or we can't afford to miss the 7.15 train to work.

So why do we worry so much—why bother? Although we profess to dislike anxiety and stress, the truth is that without them we might achieve very little. Deadlines make the world whirr round. We also have anxiety to thank for the fact that we embark upon all kinds of relationships. Small babies start finding strangers frightening at the age of a few months old. With help from their families, from babyhood to child and eventually to adolescent and adult, they gradually learn the socialising skills required to function in the culture where they live. In turn, we encounter the possibility of being a team player, being part of a working group and possibly have children of our own. All of these potentialities are measured against the possibility of assault, attack and murder. If we trust nobody, nothing much can be achieved; on the other hand, if we are too trusting, we may be lured into a trap and, in our worst fears and fantasies, embodied in the original version of *Little Red Riding Hood*, be despatched by the big bad wolf.

Each of us learns to develop skills in "reading" other people's minds, a talent that parents try to pass on to their children. Later in life, highly developed social skills are required for successful negotiation of the many pitfalls waiting in the world. As every parent knows, children are exhausting and demanding and the rewards of socialising another human being often seem far distant when toddlers are throwing tantrums and teenagers seem set against anything and everything their parents may say. Last but by no means least, living together with another human being is fraught with problems, but equally, living on ones own is often a source of misery.

* * *

There are a group of professionals who specialise in dealing with people's fantasy problems. In the clinical practices of psychoanalysts, psychotherapists and counsellors, the private fantasies of patients are a key source of material offering clues to human suffering and perhaps more optimistically, to what makes us happy. Yet, it is no accident that every day we read of the onward march of drug therapies for problems of the mind and brain. Many people would far rather take a pill to smooth out their problems with living than try to talk to someone else, even in confidence, about ideas that they often privately label with tags like "stupid", "mental" or "mad". Of course, drugs often work; but they frequently have unpleasant side effects, can be addictive and sometimes act by diminishing or cloaking the pleasant experiences of life as well as the unpleasant symptoms that led us to the doctor's surgery in the first place. Drugs in themselves only produce a limited solution to a limited range of literal questions. We can fix brains, possibly, with drugs and even more promisingly in the future with gene therapy, but can we fix our fantasies or are we about to turn ourselves into the zombies foretold of gothic horror fame—clinically alive but mindfully dead? To paraphrase Dracula, "psychiatric ways are not Transylvanian ways".

The idea that the onward march of science will somehow "reduce" human beings to machines for living is threatening to many, but if machines are created that can produce fantasies as prolifically and as usefully as human beings, would we need to fear them? I don't know. If, as seems possible, we come to believe with Richard Dawkins that humans really are an almost unbelievably sophisticated form of machine, then we will still need to find an explanation for the existence of fantasy and many of its offspring, including culture, religion and literature.

In its present form, psychoanalysis might die if the bureaucrats have everything their way. It will have to be re-invented when people find that life without free-flowing fantasy is a desperate place. This is a situation envisaged in many of the best fantasies, starkly depicted and extremely frightening. In *The Lord of the Rings* trilogy, the story starts in a homely world where anxieties are much less than those we encounter in our own daily world. The Hobbits have a very long life. They don't have to work very hard and they have plenty of time to while away much of their existence, ruminating on their good fortune in living in a place of peace and pleasant dreams. Gradually this illusion is dispelled, and, as the novel builds to a climax, the degree of anxiety that the reader is expected to tolerate slowly but surely increases. The Land of Mordor (its very name indicative of deadness and "fantasylessness") is the more dreadful because its full awfulness is only hinted at in the first two parts of the trilogy. At the end of the novel, the level of anxiety never quite returns to the untroubled beginnings of the narrative. Some of the characters have not died, but have been transported to another, more peaceful, world. The novel ends in a thoughtful and contemplative rather than an ecstatic mood.

* * *

Returning to the storyline of this book, it has three connected themes, fantasy and anxiety and the shifts in perception that each of us experiences when we try to address one with the use of the other. Anxiety spurs us to action or inhibits movement completely. Fantasy provides us with a germ of an idea, takes the sting out of agonising perceptions of our real state of mind or strands us in Never Never Land with Peter Pan. Each of us is Don Quixote.

Chapter one discusses the mechanisms involved in shifts in perception. It throws light on how we perceive ourselves, our methods of arriving at the judgements we make about our lives, particularly perhaps, in relation to those with whom we fall in love. This chapter suggests that we are all without knowing it, experienced, if often inept, dialecticians. Through constantly shifting our ground from one untenable, contradictory and intolerable idea to another, we attempt to keep our worst fantasies at bay and our anxiety levels damped down. The task of the analyst is to promote movement and shifts in our internal dialectical arguments.

The following chapter looks at what happens in the case of two relatively small groups of human beings who do not employ dialectical skills in dealing with the world. Those with a so-called "perverse" structure do not keep their worst fantasies at bay; they endlessly recycle them as imaginings that "belong to someone else, not me". The other group are those who, in the most difficult and tragic of cases, cannot separate their internal fantasising within from the exigencies of the real world outside; such people are often diagnosed as psychotic or schizophrenic. They often suffer from hallucinatory and delusional ideas about the nature of their relationship to the external world.

In the third chapter, a fundamental question is posed: what is anxiety? Does it differ from fear and does anxiety actually have some kind of object? What is the role of trauma in relation to anxiety? Do incompatible theories of trauma mean that methods employed in the consulting room should be thought through more carefully? The clinical problems of containing anxiety are discussed at some length because of the very practical issues they pose, both for the analyst and for the patient.

The fourth chapter looks at the place of the plot in fantasy both in the form of myth and in dream. What happens when we "lose the plot"? Drawing on the work of Freud, Lévi-Strauss and Lacan, it explores the idea of an underlying structure to myths and dreams. The Oedipus complex is a myth. Yet, as the work of each of these writers shows, this famous story offers truths about human experience at many levels. In its widest sense, it is at one and the same time, a true story, a response to anxiety, a means of dealing with contradiction and an emblem that articulates the progressions we make from one underlying fantasy structure to another.

Fantasies have a long literary history starting with myth and legend and then progressing with ever increasing variety to the rich cultural mix found anywhere and everywhere that supports human life. However, three literary forms vividly illuminate the relationship between anxiety and fantasy from different perspectives, gothic fantasy, science fiction and utopias. Chapter five uses examples to illustrate some surprising connections between *Northanger Abbey*, *Dracula* and *Star Trek*. How do fantasies in the culture at large interact with our private fantasy worlds?

Chapter six teases out the thread that connects the minutely detailed requirements for appropriate religious observance of Orthodox Jewry, the strident call to action, even martyrdom of some fundamentalist Muslim sects, the proselytizing zeal of American fundamentalist Christian movements, the traditional, middle-aged, middlebrow religious practice of the Church of England stalwarts and the "anything goes" philosophy of New Age movements. Is religion a special case of fantasy? Is the main purpose of religion really to fend off our anxieties rather than an act or acts of worship?

Henrik Ibsen's play, *Ghosts,* dramatizes the consequences of an organic disease that is passed on from one generation to another; the effect of syphilis on Oswald's brain and the social hypocrisies of the time are enacted through the minds of all the characters. The *meaning* of the play is located neither in the plot nor in its contents as such. *Ghosts* is a creature of the fantasies and anxieties of the characters; at the same time, it creates them. The play is the product of the interconnections of three attributes; brains, minds and bodies. If people attempt, either for the purposes of theorizing or for practical reasons, to eliminate one attribute from the equation, then, by and large, they succeed only in repressing the third term, rendering it unconscious with often undesired consequences. As both Freud and Ibsen noted, the repressed has a habit of returning.

Finally, in chapter eight, Letty arrives in the consulting room for the first time and says to Laura the analyst, "I hope this will be my last analysis." A Freudian would note the ambiguity of this statement. The end of an analysis is a hotly debated issue. Is there a real end? If we start the process of talking to an(other), does this ever stop? Yet, people wish to leave analysis often as much as they wish to be analysed. The process of fantasying continues until our death and the experience of anxiety in some form never leaves us. Since death awaits us all, some kind of ending is at hand . . .

CHAPTER ONE

Variations on a theme of negation

Once upon a time a teenage girl, Julie, meets a boy. We shall call him Joe. He becomes the love of Julie's life. Joe is a serial womaniser. He sleeps with several women in any given week whilst always declaring undying everlasting love to whoever is in his bed at the time. Over a period of twelve years Julie and Joe see each other occasionally. Julie always hopes against hope that eventually Joe will settle down with her and that together they'll live happily ever after and walk off hand in hand into the sunset.

Fifteen years later, Julie is now married to Jeremy. Julie thinks he is the ideal husband. He loves her and he is rich. Julie and Jeremy live in a nice house with a black cat called Jack. Jeremy often goes out drinking with the boys—so he says. Julie doesn't often see him in the evenings, especially during weekdays. Julie thinks that Jeremy doesn't know about her continuing love for Joe. Joe keeps her love alive by phoning once every few months to tell her that, against all the evidence, she is still the love of his life.

Julie is worried about her looks. She's reached an important birthday. James and Janice, her mother and father, have three grown-up children, Julie herself, and her brother, Johnny and the apple of their eyes, her younger sister, Jodie. Johnny has a baby and James and Janice are hoping against hope for more grandchildren. They don't mind whether it will be a Jimmy or a Jenny.

Julie doesn't like babies. They ruin your figure, and once you become a mother, Julie thinks, she won't ever be able to pretend again that she is still a teenager in love. Julie is depressed. She cries a lot when she comes to see her analyst Jackie.

W hen someone comes to analysis, they often have a story to tell like the one above. Naturally, the details differ; the gender and sexual orientation of the storyteller vary. People come in tears replete with desperation and sadness. They experience their situation as hopeless. Frequently they spend many years feeling helpless, taking antidepressants and hoping against hope that something in their external circumstances will change so that an imaginary being inside their minds will flick a switch without anyone (including themselves) having to lift a finger, or more accurately, think a new thought which would enable that switch to be flicked. Indeed the most compelling reason of all for rejecting such a thought is the fear that, lurking inside their minds is a ruthless monster waiting to flick a switch and make them howl with a mixture of pain and guilt. We will return to the contents of this story later.

* * *

The Ancient Greek philosopher Parmenides argued that the world is a static place:

Come, I shall tell you, and do you listen and convey the story,
What routes of inquiry alone there are for thinking:
The one—that [*it*] *is*, and that [*it*] *cannot not be*,
Is the path of Persuasion (for it attends upon truth);
The other—that [*it*] *is not* and that [*it*] *needs must not be*,
That I point out to you to be a path wholly unlearnable,
For you could not know what-is-not (for that is not feasible).
Nor could you point it out. (1991, p. 55)

He arrived at this conclusion using the following logic. If you pursue the path of an enquiry, something either "is" or "is not". If something "is", then Parmenides argued, it must be true. If, like Parmenides, you assume that what "is" coincides with what is true, then the negative or opposite can be rejected because it is simply untrue.

Unfortunately, life is not so simple. My fictional character, Julie, manages to believe two things at once—that she is still in love with her teenage sweetheart Joe and at the same time that she is love with her husband Jeremy. This state of affairs may of course be possible and indeed be "true". Depending upon how love is defined, she may truly be in love with more than one person at a time. However, it is just as likely that the "love" Julie experiences for each of these men are simply different figments of her imagination: the love she thinks she feels is a fantasy. The truth she experiences is not really true. But is there just one simple opposition—that which is false or "untrue"?

Thousands of people believe that astrological predictions can forecast our future, despite the lack of evidence to support these claims. One of the features of astrology that enhances its appeal is that it is impossible to show whether its predictions are true or not. Astrology asks us to believe the impossible—that, whatever the outcome of a particular event, the prediction will turn out to be true. Following in the footsteps of their distinguished predecessor, the oracle at Delphi, astrological predictions are issued in language of such ambiguity, that whatever the outcome, they can be interpreted as being "true". At one level most of us know that astrological predictions are simply comforting fantasies. At the same time many people read their horoscopes avidly and mentally jump to the conclusion that what the horoscope *really* meant was Julie is fated to divorce Jeremy and marry Joe—or perhaps to stay married to Jeremy and turn her back on Joe. In the "real" world, it is also quite likely that Julie will reject both men and go to live with a new man, Jules, or reject both men and decide to move in with Jessica. Julie may even decide to abandon close human relationships altogether and live alone with Jack the cat. Equally, in the "real" world, Julie may subscribe to Parmenides' theory and stay locked in her unhappy, frustrating and apparently inevitable world where everything stays the same.

In other words, it is striking that objectively speaking life often presents us with several possibilities, perhaps not just one "road not taken" (Frost, 1920) but several, and yet human suffering is so often about the perception that there is only one path available, often the most painful path.

There are of course several flaws in the argument of Parmenides and we will turn to these later. However, it is useful to start with this proposition, despite all its obvious faults, simply because it is so very familiar. It is the argument heard daily in the consulting room. Julie is depressed and miserable because she is convinced that her view of life is the only one available. At the same time she is often an astrological fatalist—her fate is written in the stars. Her experience of her life is something that has been "wished" upon her, it has nothing to do with her own thoughts and actions.

Is Julie's experience a permanent state of affairs or will it pass after some sessions with a therapist? From the beginning, there is a junction, a painful parting of the ways in which people start thinking. Many arrive in consulting rooms and clinics with the question: how long will it take to fix my problem? After a while, a patient says something that includes one or often all of the following general observations about the state of their existence: "My life is miserable; my partner has left; I hate my job and there isn't much point in living". After only two sessions, a patient summarised this state of affairs even more succinctly: "boring and pointless". It is notable that if considered carefully, this short phrase is itself a contradiction in terms.

If the analyst dares to query whether the facts are really as fixed and immutable as they seem, this often elicits a dogmatic, "There's no alternative". In line with the argument of Parmenides, what currently *is*, is assumed and indeed relentlessly asserted to be true. Patients arrive with a basic conflict; they believe their misery to be fixed and utterly incapable of change. At the same time they have come to see you in the hope of changing things. The grounds for their pre-existing beliefs are usually no better than the grounds for believing that ones future can be read in the stars.

If, like her patients, the analyst too stays with Parmenides, then there is no way forward. There are, however, possible routes out of this classical dilemma. Parmenides makes assumptions that can be challenged. Firstly, he assumes that something which is true now will always be true—but common sense tells us that our lives change over time. Secondly Parmenides' views are only correct if what we take to be true actually *is* true. Consequently, when faced with Parmenidean dogmatism, there is a space for questioning the apparent *status quo*. Questions, contradiction, denial and reflection over a range of possible differences and differentiations are all tools that can be brought to bear. The skill of the clinician lies in knowing which tool to apply to the apparently congealed misery presented by the patient.

Thus rather than casting the negative aside, we can use oppositions and contradictions to investigate the apparent fixity of our patients' misery. In "What is Metaphysics?" Heidegger remarks:

> The elaboration of the question of the nothing must bring us to the point where an answer becomes possible or the impossibility of any answer becomes clear. The nothing is conceded. With a studied indifference science abandons it as what "there is not."
> (Heidegger, 1978, p. 96)

Like Heidegger, we will not indifferently abandon this question. Heidegger summarises the problem very succinctly. If we ask ourselves "What is nothing?" then logically and intellectually there is no answer because there is no object available with which to answer such a question. As he says, "for the nothing is the negation of the totality of beings; it is nonbeing pure and simple."

Heidegger detects a subtle elision in this proposition. Either there has to be what he terms "a higher determination" an originary something which provides the "matter" which is negated; or, as he puts it, "is it the other way around? Are negation and the 'not' given only because nothing is given?" He continues, "that has not been decided; it has not even been raised expressly as a question. We assert that the nothing is more original than the 'not' and negation." In the example of Julie, what is the "originary something" which produces her contradictory feelings about Joe and Jeremy? Many of us fall back on the idea that it is "written in the stars" or that our lives just happen—"that's the way it is and that's all there is to it". It is noticeable that when you think of the dilemma in Heidegger's extremely abstract terms, the origin of Julie's problem is in one sense obvious, but in another, quite mysterious.

The argument then shifts to the role of the intellect in the debate about this mysterious "nothing", which continually insists on producing subtle and disturbing effects. If we take the utilitarian view that the intellect should be king and lord of the manor over everything that it surveys, then Heidegger can take us no further.

If however, we then turn to the Freudian notion of the unconscious, Heidegger's detailed analysis of the process of negation starts to become interesting. Heidegger asserts, "If the power of the intellect in the field of inquiry into the nothing and into Being is thus shattered, then the destiny of the reign of 'logic' in philosophy is thereby decided." In other words if we *don't* believe that Julie's fate is either "written in the stars" or that it "just happened this way", then we can ask ourselves some intriguing questions. This leaves the way open for us to go back in chronological time, but forward in the argument, to Freud's views on negation.

What Freud found so striking in his psychoanalytic writing was the enormous power of the intangible and ineffable—the unconscious. A simple way of thinking about Freud's work is to reflect upon the fact that we all experience a constant and subtle series of slippages—we spend our lives thinking one thing, then finding ourselves saying something rather different and finally carrying out an action which corresponds neither to our stated intention nor to our internal thoughts. No wonder people distrust the words of politicians since there are always unspoken, silent gaps between what they are prepared to say in public, what they think the electorate would like to hear, what they as individuals privately think and the policies they actually implement. What is the intangible something that produces these shifts and slippages? These slippages in our life involve us in constant conscious and unconscious contradictions.

Throughout his life Freud was preoccupied with pros and cons. Perhaps the earliest example is his interest in the work of J.S. Mill. Here is Bernard Burgoyne's account:

> Freud took up the theory of Socratic dialectic from the translation that he made in 1879 of Mill's lengthy review of the text that his friend Grote had produced on the primary importance of the technique of Socratic dialectic in the development of Greek political theory and in the development of Greek science.
>
> Grote and Mill carefully distinguished the Socratic Plato—the Plato of what they called "negative dialectics"—from the later Plato of "dogmatic" ideals. They cherished the former, and had great suspicion of the latter . . .
>
> Freud's argument is that "negative dialectic" operates on patho-logical defence, producing by its action a field of connections .

to consciousness that had been cut by the activity of defence. His early theory of defence centres round the structure of neurosis being organised round the functioning of repression. The unconscious is constructed by the ego finding certain representations intolerable, and so relegating them, hiding them away so that they are outside the domain of critical enquiry. (Burgoyne, 2000, p. 197)

To translate this explanation into the terms of Julie's problem, Julie has one argument in her mind that tells her that Joe is the love of her life; she has another equally powerful argument that tells her that Jeremy is the ideal husband. These ideas cannot both be true at the same time except through a very clever sleight of hand, or perhaps more accurately, through a series of ingenious mental acrobatics. The "Joe idea" and the "Jeremy idea" are each relegated in turn to the unconscious. In the process, the conscious mind is kept so busy on this endless treadmill of exchanging one mutually contradictory idea for another, that the much more alarming prospect of having a baby is safely lost from view most of the time. Julie's analyst, Jackie, can start to suspect that these ideas are in circulation by observing a curious fact. Whenever words like "mummy", "mothering" and "baby" crop up in the conversation, Julie suddenly stops in her tracks: Julie says, "I don't want to talk about this." Why not? It is as if the conversation has suddenly touched a raw nerve. The direct reference to something that until now has been apparently safely tucked away in the unconscious, produces a sudden sharp spurt of anxiety into what Julie normally experiences as her rather flat and slightly depressed emotional landscape.

The theme of the negative is one that appears again and again in Freud's work. In 1893 in *Studies in Hysteria* Freud and Breuer discuss the concept of negative hallucination, in Breuer's case study of Anna O. In brief, "negative hallucination" is the experience of being unable to see what is staring you in the face. Here is Bernard Burgoyne's illustration of this phenomenon.

Let us suppose that I am standing in front of an audience. There is a table immediately in front of me. I hypnotise a member of the audience and inform them that when they wake up they will

*not see the table. When they wake, I ask this person to hand me
a book that is on the floor immediately beyond the table.*

*What will happen when I ask this person to pass me the book?
Will they bump into the table? Will they walk round it? What
will they say if I ask them to explain their action?*

*The hypnotised person will make a detour around the table
and offer apparently plausible explanations for their action—"well
there was a sudden draft from the window" or "I was distracted
by a noise coming from the audience". If I ask them is there was
anything in the room which prevented them coming straight
towards me to hand over the book, they will answer in the
negative.*

In other words, consciously, you will not see the table in front of
you, but unconsciously you will take account of this fact and produce
a rationalisation—a false explanation—for your actions. This is a very
curious phenomenon. At one and the same time, in one sense, the
hypnotised person "knows" that there is something in the way; in
another, they are ignorant of the existence of the table. Thus, Julie
"knows" that she is unhappy. She "knows" two contradictory things
about Joe and Jeremy. What Julie *doesn't* know, although it is obvious
to her analyst Jackie, is that she is so terrified of having children that
she is prepared to keep her unrealistic views of Joe and Jeremy in a
state of constant unhappy tension so that with luck(?) she'll never
have to become pregnant.

Perhaps the above sounds familiar. When patients are confronted
with the contradiction between one statement and another about their
lives, they usually produce endless rationalisations. Julie thinks
that she is forever stuck with a "Mexican stand off" between Joe
and Jeremy. Her first rationalisation is that nothing can change. Her
second rationalisation is that her dilemma is a repetition of her
mother Janice's experience. Julie says that Janice really loved another
man called Joseph but settled for security and money and married
James instead. Julie cannot see that her depression and sadness
mainly come from her *own* attitudes to her life, not from those around
her—she is suffering from a negative hallucination. It takes much
hard work to allow someone to perceive even a small fraction of a
"more truthful" relationship between themselves and the other,
whether this other is a person, a table or indeed figments of one's

imagination. Normally people become very inventive if they suspect that someone such as an analyst is getting anywhere near to putting a finger on any of the anxieties that they have unwittingly taken so much trouble to conceal. In analysis Julie is likely to produce many more rationalisations, each of which may contain a germ of "truth" but which really function as red herrings to lead both the analyst and Julie away from the seat of anxiety. Thus, Julie's story about her mother Janice's previous love is probably true, but it is not necessarily anything more than simply part of a much more complicated series of interlocking, often contradictory, "reasons". Freud calls this phenomenon of attempting to avoid unpleasant truths about one's life, "resistance".

Freud's brief essay "Negation" (1925) is a mine of further fascinating and useful information for shedding light on Julie's dilemma. Here is the second paragraph of the essay to illustrate what I mean:

> There is a very convenient method by which we can sometimes obtain a piece of information we want about unconscious repressed material. "What", we ask, "would you consider the most unlikely imaginable thing in that situation? What do you think was furthest from your mind at that time?" If the patient falls into the trap and says what he thinks is most incredible, he almost always makes the right admission. A neat counterpart to this experiment is often met with in an obsessional neurotic who has already been initiated into the meaning of his symptoms. "I've got a new obsessive idea," he says, "and it occurred to me at once that it might mean so and so. But no; that can't be true, or it couldn't have occurred to me." What he is repudiating, on the grounds picked up from his treatment, is, of course, the correct meaning of the obsessive idea. (Freud, 1925h, p. 235)

As Freud indicates, the content of a repressed idea *can* find its way into consciousness, if it is negated—in Heideggerian terminology, it becomes "nothing". If we assume for the sake of argument, that Julie is an obsessional neurotic, we might rudely and quite possibly unwisely, interrupt her complaints about Joe and Jeremy and ask her to reply to Freud's questions, "What would you consider the most unlikely imaginable thing in that situation? What do you think was furthest from your mind at that time?" Any answer that included some reference to her problems having nothing to do with babies, or perhaps how much she loves her brother Johnny's new daughter, Jasmine, would confirm Freud's view.

People make unconscious judgements about their own lives; in other words, they take a very particular, idiosyncratic and often grossly erroneous view of their own experiences. The work of the analysis is to subject these judgements to scrutiny. A theory of judgement is a key part of Freud's explanation of negation, viz, ". . . the performance of the function of judgement is not made possible until the creation of the symbol of negation has endowed thinking with a first measure of freedom from the consequences of repression, and, with it, from the compulsion of the pleasure principle" (Freud, 1925h, p. 239). Freud's argument, then, is that if Jackie is to try to help Julie, her task has to be addressed to the problem of the seemingly bizarre judgements that Julie constructs for herself in order to keep her anxiety at bay. For example, Julie's view is that Joe can be "the love of her life" even if he only contacts her two or three times a year; why does Julie have such an enormous emotional investment in someone who treats her so casually?

The role of the question becomes a key piece in this complicated game of emotional chess being conducted by the analyst Jackie and the patient Julie. Perhaps it is a good idea to summarise some of Julie's "moves" so far, before tackling this issue:

(a) Julie allows as little change, difference or movement as possible into her life;

(b) Julie suffers emotionally;

(c) Before any change, variation, or movement can be perceived, a registration of difference has to take place in Julie's mind;

(d) Difference is often registered as negation—Julie "loves" Joe and Jeremy in different ways, each "love" contradicting or negating the other;

(e) In the unconscious, there is no registration of difference and therefore no negation—so Julie is unaware of this contradiction;

(f) However, in the conscious world, a small modicum of difference is tolerated—Julie knows that she is unhappy and that it has something to do with love;

(g) Thus, negation offers the halfway house of admitting something to consciousness but only in its negated form. As Freud
says of a patient's reported dream at the beginning of the
Negation paper, "'It's *not* my mother', we emend this to:
'So it *is* his mother.' . . . It is as though the patient had said:
'It's true that my mother came into my mind as I thought of
this person, but I don't feel inclined to let the association
count.'" (Freud, 1925h, p. 235). Thus Julie might say, "it's true
that my brother's baby, Jasmine came to mind, but I don't
really think that's at all important."

(h) Keeping the *really* unpleasant ideas of pregnancy at bay by
ensuring that they are always camouflaged by a constantly
moving series of contradictory statements in her mind about
Joe and Jeremy keeps Julie away from the feared precipice of
tumbling into a state of complete terror—something unknown
and beyond Julie's imagination;

(i) The reality of pregnancy, if it were to happen to Julie, might
or might not increase the anxiety she currently experiences.
It would be likely to shift her pattern of contradictory anxieties
into a new pattern, making use of some old ideas, shedding
others and introducing fresh sources of anxiety, particularly
of course, those that emanate from the baby.

This list is by no means exhaustive but it gives a snapshot of some
of the ideas likely to be a source of constant preoccupation for Julie.
We are now shifting from the motionless position of Parmenides.
What is opening up is the notion that although someone's life may
appear to be static, stasis is induced by the conflicting demands of
the unconscious. The result is anxiety in myriad forms *plus* a kind
of permanent unhappy tension between a series of contradictory
ideas. Julie's experience is a little like an elastic band being kept in
a state of maximum tension, pulled in a series of different directions
at the same time. The conflicting impulses cancel each other out
leaving someone like Julie in a state where they feel incapable of
changing anything about their lives. If Jackie attempts to intervene,
however cautiously, it may feel to Julie that even the slightest
disturbance will run the risk of breaking the elastic band rather than
reducing the tension.

The problem of the unconscious/lack of knowledge/not knowing/ the nothing cannot simply be ignored and discounted. As we know to our cost, our emotional problems do not usually go away if we try to ignore them. Freud argues that the theory of judgement can be applied as follows: when the patient asserts that *in their own view* nothing can change, then the analyst Jackie, can ask a series of questions, provoking the patient into querying their own presumed-to-be-correct judgements. In fact, Jackie does not always even need to ask questions. Julie may find that, in the process of talking about her problems, it starts to occur to her that what she is saying does not add up. In other words, with the help of the analyst's silence, Jackie has the opportunity to wonder about what she is really saying. Does her love for Joe exist in reality? Is Jeremy in fact the perfect husband?

The lack of negation in the unconscious may be true but as we have seen, the function of judgement applied in the preconscious, (a Freudian no-man's-land between the conscious and the unconscious) results in a conflict in consciousness between two or more apparently incompatible ideas. Jackie has a problem on her hands. If she persuades Julie to start questioning her apparently fixed feelings for Joe and Jeremy, what will happen? Julie may find that even a slight shift in her fixed ideas means that the spectre of pregnancy becomes unbearable and leaves her with her views about Joe and Jeremy untouched and thus with her fear of pregnancy unaddressed. If Jackie is a Kleinian analyst, she might choose to take the direct route and tackle the North face of the Eiger; Jackie might offer Julie a view that her unhappiness about Joe and Jeremy is really a cover for her primitive feelings of terror about childbirth. The problem with the direct route is that while it may address the anxiety, it will not necessarily disrupt the complex organisation of contradictory ideas that is a concomitant of the anxiety. If Jackie is a Lacanian analyst, she might take the view that an occasional intervention which plays on Julie's equivocations might be a better route. This kind of intervention can be theorised as a calculus where the latter is a formal set of (mathematical) rules of a language applied to *changing quantities* to determine the value of its functions. Natalie Charraud illustrates this approach when analysing an intervention made in a session with one of her own patients,

"There's rejection" kept open all the ambiguities, whilst not brushing aside the object of rejection. In particular, my statement played on the equivocation introduced by the terms which arranged themselves around this signifying term. (Charraud, 2000, p. 219)

The appearance of more than one idea may produce suffering, but at the same time, it offers an opportunity and a space for questions. The problem with this approach could be that years later, the analyst might still be wandering around in the foothills of Julie's problem— or then again this method might prove extremely effective. Patients are often experts at keeping the prospect of change at bay—a situation Fairbairn theorises as a "balancing act" between the exciting and the rejecting egos (Fairbairn, 1952, p. 105).

* * *

The argument does not end here however. If we allow negation a space or perhaps an absence, then what are the consequences that follow from the questions that may be asked of this space or absence? We mentioned Socratic dialectics earlier in this chapter. What is the impact of dialectics on human suffering? And indeed, is there a place for considering the role of dialectics in the structuring of fantasy? This argument bring us back to the role of the question that I introduced prior to listing the patient's moves in the analytical game of chess so far. We shall now take a look at the repertoire of moves (again by no means exhaustive) available to Jackie the analyst:

(a) As we have indicated above, Julie's thought patterns may go round in circles, in which case a question is often an effective way of breaking into this self-referential trap;

(b) Jackie might try linking a word or phrase with a similar or linked word or phrase from elsewhere in the session or perhaps with something Julie said even many months earlier; this new link may then put Julie in touch with issues that were previously unavailable to her;

(c) Jackie can sit in silence. As I indicated above, Julie might be the kind of patient who needs to use the space for thinking;

(d) By now, Julie may think that she knows what analysis is all about and what to expect—so Jackie may change her style a little—for example, by talking more, rather than less (or *vice versa*). She may change the type of comments she normally makes; this can have the effect of gently shifting Julie away from well-worn ways of thinking that have become habitual rather than helpful;

(e) If Jackie is a Lacanian analyst she may vary the length of the session, "punctuating" it by bringing it to a close at a moment when Jackie deems there is the possibility of Julie being gently jolted into a new way of thinking about her problems.

It is worth noting that each of the ideas in Jackie's repertoire either involves asking a question, provoking Julie to ask a question, or perhaps leaving Julie to wonder what she is thinking about. The essence of a dialectic is its shifting nature—there is always another question. Answers are in short supply; however, if one looms on the horizon, then patients start to contemplate not only their depression and sadness but also the nature of what they usually view as a kind of loss.

We can use a famous Freudian illustration here. In his account of his grandson's "fort-da" game, Freud puts forward the notion that a major part of the experience of being human is coping with the complex feelings of yearning and longing that come from absence, lack, loss, or simply a sensation of incompleteness.

> This good little boy, . . . had an occasional disturbing habit of taking any small objects he could get hold of and throwing them away from him into a corner, under the bed, and so on . . . As he did this he gave vent to a loud, long-drawn-out "o-o-o-o" accompanied by an expression of interest and satisfaction. His mother and the writer of the present account were agreed in thinking that this was not a mere interjection but represented the German word *"fort"* ["gone"] . . . The child had a wooden reel with a piece of string tied round it . . . What he did was to hold the reel by the string and very skilfully throw it over the edge of his curtained cot, so that it disappeared into it, at the same time uttering his expressive "o-o-o-o". He then pulled the reel out of the cot again by the string and hailed its reappearance with a joyful *"da"* ["there"]. (Freud, 1920g, p. 15)

Freud's interpretation of this game was that the child was able to bear his mother's absence by using the game of disappearance (absence) followed by reappearance (imaginary presence). Freud proposes that the mechanism through which the substitution of the throwing and retrieval of the reel for the absence and return of the mother is achieved by the substitution of the passive situation of having to tolerate absence with the active process of the game. Implicitly, therefore, Julie's "Mexican stand-off" situation outlined above is resolved by changing her experience from "passive" into "active". It is worth noting, however, that the child/Julie still have to deal with the suffering caused by the mother/imaginary lover"s absence. The price of keeping anxiety at bay is the substitution of the anxiety of loss with a fantasy involving retrieval—the cotton reel/Julie's wish that she will walk off into the sunset with Joe hand in hand and live happily ever after.

The question then arises: what is it that the child/Julie has really lost? At this stage in his life, the mother of the real child whom Freud was describing was still alive; she was absent for a few hours but by no means gone forever. (Sadly, as Freud reports in a footnote to this story, the child's mother [Freud's daughter] died when he was five and three-quarters). Lacan explores the phenomena of loss, lack and the multiplicity of fantasies surrounding these experiences and the reasons for his continued interest in this topic are obvious in the clinical context. When patients like Julie seek analysis, statements such as "My life is miserable; my partner has left; I hate my job and there isn't much point in living" are redolent of experiences of lack and loss.

Lacan uses a phrase, the "object a", the object cause of desire, in multiple ways to describe that which cannot be symbolised but which causes us to make the substitution so well described by Freud in the "fort-da" game. The object a is the Scarlet Pimpernel of human experience; or in the words of the Kinks' song "Dedicated Follower of Fashion"

They seek him here, they seek him there,
In Regent Street and Leicester Square.
Everywhere the Carnabetian army marches on,
Each one a dedicated follower of fashion.

The "dedicated follower of fashion" never arrives *at* fashion. This is but one example of an experience found in many walks of life. We pursue something like fashion with the ultimate aim of being right up to the minute. However we can never attain a state that is more than roughly thirty seconds before this "minute" comes to fruition. When we are close to this achievement, we look back over our shoulders to check that nobody has run past us whilst we are striving to reach the goal. This moment of hesitation induces doubt and the goal eludes us once more.

However, we need to trace our steps back from doubt for a moment and return to Julie's story. If Julie is "in love" with Joe and also "in love" with Jeremy at the same time, she cannot have James' and Janice's much longed-for second grandchild. Joe is hardly there long enough to conceive a child, but if Julie does conceive (as she has done in the past) then she has an abortion because she knows that Joe won't support her. Her fantasy of walking off into the sunset with him is in ruins. If she stays married to Jeremy then she finds it difficult to have sex at all with him because she feels she is abandoning Joe and being unfaithful to him. The analyst might ask herself (and possibly Julie) the question: who is really doing the abandoning here? Yet, Julie describes Jeremy as "the ideal husband". The two fantasies are interdependent and maintain Julie in a state of permanent depression. She can never have what she thinks she wants.

Thus, another puzzle starts to emerge. At the start of her analysis, Julie remarked that she needed to sort out her love life because she is getting older and she wants to have a baby. Why then does Julie have abortions? If she really wanted a baby, she earns enough to ditch both Joe and Jeremy and live on her own with Jack the cat and either baby Jimmy or baby Jenny. Even though she is frequently in tears over her unhappy love life, Julie has slumbering, often unspoken, deeper anxieties. She is terrified that a baby would mean that she could no longer be the teenager in love. She is fearful of an unwitting repetition of her mother's marked indifference to her as the elder daughter and her painful preference even now, when Julie has reached thirty, for the younger daughter, Jodie.

Enter the interesting Freudian notion of secondary gain—does Julie get anything from this experience apart from a bottomless well of tears? When Jackie the analyst draws Julie's attention to words like "mother" and "baby", then Julie's reaction is surprising. At one level, She *really really* doesn't want a baby. Julie gains relief from her anxiety about being a mother so long as her intertwined fantasies about Joe and Jeremy persist. It is now possible to start teasing out a pattern in Julie's suffering. The people that she thinks she loves the most, Joe and Jeremy, are really figments of her imagination as well as being "real people" at the same time. Freud's concept of secondary gain—"accepting" one group of fears in order to ward off and conceal an even greater anxiety—is therefore clearly at work in Julie's case.

Freud's own examples of this phenomenon come from rather more dramatic clinical sources. He says:

> . . . [T]he severe tremors which give pronounced cases of these [war] neuroses a similarity that is so striking at the first glance, as well as apprehensiveness, tearfulness, and a proneness to fits of rage, accompanied by convulsive infantile motor manifestations, and to vomiting ("at the least excitement").

> . . . [A] remark made by an acquaintance in the street—"you look in really excellent form, you're certainly fit now"—is enough to produce an immediate attack of vomiting. (Freud, 1901b, p. 115)

Here Freud's example of war neurosis adds another dimension to our story—the role of trauma and its relation to nightmare and fantasy. Thus, Julie may also have traumatic reasons for not wanting baby Jenny or baby Jimmy. The topic of trauma and its close connection to anxiety and the "stopping in its tracks" of fantasy is one of the subjects of chapter three.

If Julie is really going to have a baby, then her analyst Jackie may have to help her intervene in the otherwise never interrupted grinding treadmill of her fantasies. If this chapter reads like a meditation on a constantly recurring theme reiterating the same idea in different ways, this may give a flavour of Julie's problems. At the beginning of this chapter, I referred to "flicking a switch". A rather crude summary of the argument outlined above might be that fantasies can be "switched on and off" or perhaps they might be imagined as operating like a flickering light occasionally illuminating a small otherwise dark corner of our field of perception. There are some fantasies however, that are full of pain, from which we flinch—more like a ruthless overseer flicking a switch to keep the prisoners working hard at their useless task of breaking up stones. Julie's mother Janice has always made Julie feel that however well she does at work and however hard she slaves away in the competitive world of IT consultancy, this is irrelevant compared to being happily married and having babies. For others this might be problematic but not traumatic: but in Julie's case, this conflict between her aspirations and her mother's expectations is literally unbearable—even unthinkable. In the next chapter we will look the experiences of those who do not employ negative dialectics at all, but develop radically different solutions to the problem of anxiety.

CHAPTER TWO

Other minds, other worlds

Xanthe, a psychoanalytic psychotherapist, is in private practice and advertises her services in the telephone directory. One day the phone rings and when she picks it up she hears a man's voice.
    "Do you have time to talk to me?", X enquires.
    "Are you responding to my advertisement?", she replies.
    "Yes, I thought you might be interested in my problem."
    "Can you perhaps tell me something about this?"
    "Well, I don't know if you really want to know what I've got to tell you. It's about me and my girlfriend." He lowers his voice to a suggestive tone, *"We love each other very much but when it comes to having sex, she doesn't want to do the things I want to do . . ."*

If allowed to continue, this kind of conversation will often become more and more sexually explicit and later the sounds of masturbation will be heard over the phone. Whether Xanthe terminates the call at the point reached above or waits for the caller to reach orgasm and then in all likelihood slam down the phone, Xanthe will probably never know the name of X or the nature of his "problem".

Telephone help lines receive many such calls and have to train their staff to deal with them. Being on the receiving end of such a call is a memorably unpleasant experience. It evokes anxiety in the listener whereas the caller sounds as if he is enjoying himself. Staff who regularly "woman" telephone help lines make the following kinds of observations. Callers of this kind always tell the same story, frequently using identical turns of phrase each time. Most, but not all, are men and they prefer wherever possible to speak to a woman whom they do not expect to participate in their sexual fantasy; however, they do require her to be present in the role of a passive listener.

The world of perversion

The dialectical theme of chapter one was developed on the premise that people deal with anxiety by negating and repressing it. Neurotics try to push uncomfortable and contradictory ideas under the carpet by repressing them; they then have to deal with the resultant internal and external conflicts that escape from repression. There are others, however, who deal with anxiety by inducing it in others, often in the manner described in the vignette above. There is no dialectical engagement here. As in Julie's story, this vignette includes fantasy and anxiety—but there the similarity ends. There are several differences from the neurotic model that can be gleaned from X's interchange with Xanthe. Here the anxiety, instead of being repressed, has been diverted onto Xanthe, the listener. X is enabled to feel at ease with himself because any anxiety he might have originally felt is completely disowned. It has been "transferred" to Xanthe, the therapist, who is saddled with "the problem" (provided she does not put the phone down when she realises what is happening). X is attempting to eject his anxiety into Xanthe. However, this is not a permanent solution. X needs to keep repeating the same formulaic fantasy as listeners on phone help lines will attest. Why does the repetition need to be so precise and why do people like X phone help lines in the first place? What kind of "help" (if any) do they need? It is noticeable that questions like these do not promote a yearning for answers. X is not really interested in Xanthe's response to his problem. He simply wants an audience. The only possibility of release for X is a form of "mindless" repetition of a fantasy that does not engage him in thinking about it, leading eventually to ejaculation—a bodily reaction. The pervert's fantasy is notable for its lack of originality. The sexual act is shorn of variety, surprise and humour. As the vignette above hints, it is a one-sided affair since the listener is not expected to actively participate in any way and the sexual act usually consists in masturbation—having sex with oneself.

The numbers of people who actually behave in the manner described above are not numerous, but they can sometimes have a high profile in the news. Some paedophiles operate in the manner described. It is noticeable that such people rarely feel ashamed of their actions. If no dialectic is set up, then the difference between one kind of behaviour and another and its concomitant effect on others will not (and cannot) be acknowledged. A psychoanalyst might understand such behaviour as indicative of an underlying, often unconscious, structure and describe such people in terms of possessing a perverse structure, rather than the dialectically engaged neurotic one described in the previous chapter.

A popular current psychiatric and psychological term for perverse actions is "paraphilia". It is used to denote any form of sexual fantasying that involves deviation from what are considered to be current societal norms. However, this can be misleading. Although paraphilia is used as a diagnostic term, it cannot account for the distinction between perverse fantasies and perverse acts, in other words the difference between thinking about something and carrying it out. Whilst traditionally named "perverts" and/or paedophiles are clearly included in this definition, more controversially, those of us who have a more "normal" neurotic structure may indulge in these practices too; in terms of our private inner thoughts, who has never had a "perverse" fantasy?

Perversion is a term often traditionally associated with so-called "dirty old men" like X in the vignette at the beginning of this chapter. Paedophilia, sexual abuse and indeed any sexual habit that is regarded by the majority of members of a particular culture as deviant are often deemed to be perverse. This leads to a whole series of problems of terminology as more and more people are "included" or "excluded" at the stroke of a pen. Version II of the Diagnostic Statistical Manual (DSM) decided that homosexuality was a perversion, psychiatrically speaking, largely because it was seen to be a variant of the dominant sexual practice in most cultures. As a result of public outcry, the definition was removed three years later.

Perversion in the sense in which X deliberately sets out to disturb the thinking of his listener is clearly an entirely different proposition from the activities of homosexuals, many of whom have no interest whatever in arousing anxiety in their partners or anyone else! The creation of anxiety in another is one of the keys to understanding the perverse structure. People are frightened of perverts; people are frightened of anyone who is "different" from them; therefore, the thinking goes—all people who are different from "us" are perverts. This is the logic of the popular press. More disturbingly, it is often the logic of the well-informed. An unacknowledged and difficult aspect of perversion is that, while it is often disgusting and revolting—sexual abuse is both of these things—it can also have an underbelly of illicit attraction. Pornographic websites are amongst the few that are regularly profitable on the internet and the storylines of soaps abound with every possible sexual variation, which if not actually depicted, are described in explicit language.

There is a further structural difference between neurosis and perversion, which turns on the distinctively different relationship of the subject to the other in perversion as distinct from neurosis. Neurotics are concerned to change the way others perceive them and their world. Those with a perverse structure are indifferent to the thoughts and feelings of others. In the vignette, the lack of empathy and awareness of any moral dilemma on the part of X is very striking.

Splitting occurs in perversion as well as in neurosis. In perversion, however, anxiety is always split in the same way. Instead of producing several, ever changing, contradictory attitudes towards an anxiety-provoking idea, perverts split off their anxiety and vest it in its entirety in "the other". "The other" is nothing other than the disowned and disavowed aspect of their own anxiety. In perversion, splitting operates as a closed loop. Paradox in the pervert is situated in a different "place" from the "place" of paradox in the neurotic. The neurotic situates herself firmly on the horns of her dilemma, . . . shall I, shan't I . . . In the pervert's life there is apparently no "other" at all: it has been pushed away into another person or place. Yet it still remains in the commitment of the perverse unconscious to endless unvarying repetition.

Thus far, perversion has been discussed in terms of its structural relationship to anxiety. However, it also has a connection to fantasy. Lacan's account of the distinction and relationship between fantasy and perversion as structures is illuminating. He uses two self-evidently related formulae as follows:

$S <> a$ is his formula for fantasy

$a <> S$ is his formula for perversion

where S is the divided subject (a human being viewed from the subjective as distinct from the objective position) and a is the object cause of desire. These formulae summarise Lacan's observation that, in fantasy, a person is constantly pursuing an elusive definition of something that excites and/or troubles him. At the same time, the process of pursuit takes his mind away from the anxiety generated by this "something" and a fantasy is generated. In the case of perversion, however, there is no room for fantasising. Anxiety is expelled (in fantasy at least). The price paid by the pervert is the fate of remaining on the endless treadmill of "mindless" repetition. Perverse fantasies tend to be limited and limiting. They are not limited to the pervert however; neurotics often make use of them too. It is one of the reasons why pornography (mainly but not solely consumed by men) is so predictable—and also why Mills & Boon fantasies (aimed principally at the female market) are written to a fixed formula.

The notion of perverse fantasy is extensively explored in the voluminous writings of the Marquis de Sade. His collected works run to some sixteen volumes. Perhaps this is no accident, since, as I have already indicated, one of the characteristics of perversion is the tendency to apparently inexhaustible and endless repetition. Unless one is in thrall to a particular pornographic image, it becomes one big yawn.

Angela Carter explores the cultural, including the psychoanalytic, significance of de Sade's work in *The Sadeian Woman*, a book that is memorably lacking in perverse characteristics, since she is succinct, witty and decisive in her opinions. She compares de Sade's two heroines, the sisters Justine and Juliette:

> The sisters exist in a complex dialectic with one another; the experience of one makes plain the experience of the other. The innocent Justine is punished by a law she believes is just; the crime-soiled Juliette is rewarded because she undermines the notion of justice on which the law is allegedly based. (Carter, 1979, p. 103)

However, what is striking about the dialectical engagement of the masochistic Justine and the sadistic Juliette is the lack of external referents in Sade's extended perverse fantasying. They are emblems, props of fantasy, not real people—fantasies within fantasies. As Carter says, "Justine is the holy virgin; Juliette is the profane whore" (Carter, 1979, p. 101). The dialectical engagement never references the other as the equal and opposite fantasy in the internal world of the pervert except at the level of the unconscious.

Psychosis: another dialectical absence

If the perverse structure results in diminishing returns for fantasy, there is a third structure where, in one sense fantasy is rampant, but in another, it has no room for existence at all.

Freud's classic account of psychosis is to be found in his case study based on the memoirs of a hitherto successful German judge, Daniel Paul Schreber who experienced a psychotic breakdown (Freud, 1911c). There are two persuasive reasons for returning to Freud once more. Firstly, Schreber was treated in an age before the invention of psychotropic drugs changed the nature of the hallucinations commonly experienced by psychotic patients. Secondly, Schreber's *Memoirs of My Nervous Illness* (2000 [1903]) are an extraordinarily lucid account of his experience of severe mental illness. During its course, he managed to write notes, maintaining a constant account of his subjective experiences. He then assembled them into a short book with the above title. From Schreber's point of view, the purpose of the *Memoirs* was to demonstrate to a court of law that he no longer needed to be held against his will in an asylum. He was temporarily successful; as a result of the court case, he was released—only for his illness to recur in 1907 and result in his rehospitalisation until his death in 1911.

In the introduction to the *Memoirs*, Schreber starts by describing in conventional terms the reasons for writing them. He comments rather disarmingly that, "It is ... necessary to give ... the circle of my acquaintances, an approximate idea at least of my religious conceptions, so that they may have some understanding of the necessity which forces me to various oddities of behaviour ..." (1903, p. 15). What unfolds is a detailed account of hallucinatory delusions.

Schreber adhered to a complicated system of religious beliefs, which, he claimed, influenced and affected not only his thought but also his body. He subscribed to the view that his body was being turned into that of a woman; this was effected by a complicated system of rays. Real figures such as his doctor Flechsig, figures from religions such as Ariman, Ormuzd and Jehovah were all conflated with figures of his own invention, not real people, but "fleeting-improvised men" (1903, p. 40 and elsewhere). At times, Schreber attempts differentiation, for example between an upper god (Ariman) and a lower god (Ormuzd) (p. 30 and elsewhere). However, such differentiation never leads anywhere. Although on occasion a chapter refers to new developments in his thinking, these new developments do not change his attitude to the world. However misguided and incoherent the thoughts of a neurotic may be, those of a psychotic appear to be completely directionless. The discourse of a psychotic has a hypnotic quality. The endless repetitions and dead ends remind one of the mesmerising speech of demagogues such as Hitler, un-wittingly anticipated by Freud in his chapter on hypnosis at the end of *Group Psychology and the Analysis of the Ego* (Freud, 1921c). The demagogue hypnotises his audience so that they ignore their own ego and listen only to the ego ideal, the fantasy vision presented to them in alluringly simplistic and repetitive terms.

Here is Schreber attempting a hypnotic dialectical argument in his *Memoirs*:

Even now I would count it a great triumph for my dialectical dexterity if through the present essay, which seems to be grow-ing to the size of a scientific work, I should achieve only *the one* result, to make the physicians shakes their heads in doubt as to whether after all there was some truth in my so-called delu-sions and hallucinations . . . Added to this I thought during my early stay in this Asylum that the physicians themselves were only fleeting-improvised-men and that their deliberations were influenced by the rays hostile to me—a notion, the latter part of which in any case, I must still maintain as correct, however little the physicians, in the nature of the matter, will realize it themselves. (Schreber, 2000 [1903] ft., p. 129 italics in the original)

Analysing the text above, there are a number of logical fallacies that come to light. If Schreber construes his writing as an exercise in "dialectical dexterity", then how could there be only one result if his delusions and hallucinations are true? If they *are* true then there needs to be an account *either*, of *differentiated* delusions and hallucinations *or*, ideas which do not conform to the concept of a delusion or a hallucination. If they *are not* true, then there needs to be an account of what it is to cause the "physicians to shake their heads *in doubt*" (my italics).

In psychosis, splitting from "the other" is attempted, but never ultimately allowed to take place. In his early work, the "Psycho-Neuroses of Defence", (Freud, 1894a), Freud suggested that the presence or absence of hallucination was a key factor in distinguishing between neurosis and psychosis. Here is his account:

> The fact to which I now wish to call attention is that the content of a hallucinatory psychosis of this sort *consists precisely in the accentuation of the idea* which was threatened by the precipitating cause of the onset of the illness. One is therefore justified in saying that the ego has fended off the incompatible idea through a flight into psychosis. The process by which this has been achieved once more eludes the subject's self-perception, as it eludes psychologico-clinical analysis. . . . The ego breaks away from the incompatible idea; but the latter is inseparably connected with a piece of reality, so that, in so far as the ego achieves this result, it, too, has detached itself wholly or in part from reality. In my opinion this latter event is the condition under which the subject's ideas receive the vividness of hallucinations; and thus when the defence has been successfully carried out he finds himself in a state of hallucinatory confusion. (1894a, pp. 59–60, italics in the original)

Notably Freud stresses in the passage above the notion of the "accentuation" in contradistinction to the differentiation of an idea. At the heart of the psychotic process is the notion of the lack of distinction between the ego and the outside world.

A year later, in draft H of his letters to Wilhelm Fliess, Freud produced a table indicating that hallucination is a characteristic of psychosis and furthermore, the table indicates that hysterical psychosis has a *failure* of defence as its outcome. This has crucial implications for psychotic fantasy. Putting it in Lacanian terms, The Symbolic register, which includes the reference to the other and thereby provides meaning to an interchange, is missing because of the failure to make the differentiation between what is real in the sense of belonging to reality, and what is fantasy. Neurotics are often deluded but at an unconscious level at least, they *know* they are deluded. On the other hand, someone suffering from a psychotic hallucination cannot distinguish this state from external reality. Neurotics suffering from a hangover and blearily drinking a cup of tea from a cup decorated with spots may delusionally *think* that the spots are dancing on the teacups; psychotics *know* with hallucinatory certainty that the spots *are* dancing on the teacups. Fantasy and external reality are indistinguishable.

The second part of the text then suggests that the hallucination lies in Schreber's physicians—they are "only fleeting-improvised-men". Hallucination is built upon hallucination, since the deliberations of the physicians are "influenced by rays hostile to me". A dialectical process is not taking place here, rather a process of attempted fusion—one result—and a process of accretion whereby one hallucination is used to support the otherwise untenable proposition of another—a second result. Fusion and accretion do not result in a dialectical engagement, since one process has no necessary influence or connection with the other.

For our purposes, the key questions are: are these psychotic hallucinations a form of fantasy? If they are a form of fantasy, then what, if any is their relationship to the anxiety felt by psychotics? Finally is the distinction between the illusory qualities of neurotic fantasying on a continuum with the delusions of psychosis and therefore the boundaries are blurred, or are such states indicative of underlying psychic structures that are in essence mutually exclusive? Opinion on this issue is divided in the psychoanalytic world. On the one hand, Melanie Klein and her followers are of the opinion that we all have the capacity to think like Schreber—we are all "a little mad" occasionally, particularly at times of stress. For Lacan however, the structure of psychosis and neurosis is such that the means of thinking in each are largely mutually exclusive. After early childhood when, in Freudian terms we have negotiated (or not) the inevitable diminishing of our omnipotence that is implied by the passage of the infant through the Oedipus complex, the possibilities of theorising our relationship to the world radically differently moves from "close to impossible" to—literally—"unthinkable".

Of all the possible forms of human emotional suffering, psychosis is amongst the most distressing to witness. Schreber's delusional system is unique to him. His certainty of the truth of his experience is largely driven by the wish at all costs to avoid acknowledging that he is utterly alone in his deluded understanding of his world. Whilst each of us has our own belief system, most of us can share at least some aspects of our thinking with others. The loneliest people on earth are psychotics. The fantasies themselves are interesting; they clearly torture Schreber, but, at the same time, he feels that he could not do without them since they are the only "people" in his world. In fact, this ambivalent attitude towards his suffering offers perhaps the only hope of a differentiation that might lead to change. However, this is soon dashed by the perception that Schreber has no effective means of distinguishing between pleasure, and relief from pain and punishment—and thereby from torture itself.

Colin MacCabe's introduction to Andrew Webber's recent retranslation of Freud's Schreber case aptly summarises the distinctive nature of psychotic fantasy:

The psychotic has never accepted the real sociality of language, that which makes of his existence a mere link in the chain, because the father instead of introducing him to lack has held out the promise of an all-powerful existence. If the mother has been taken away from him, subtracted by her desire for another, the father promises to be cause of his own desire. The psychotic then never really uses language. Schreber's text is strikingly free of metaphor, the fundamental trope where we find ourselves transformed in language, just as it is almost completely free of femininity. (Freud, 2002, p. xvi)

Fantasy, in the hands of a psychotic is characterised by absences. Connections between one part of a psychotic's fantasy life and another have to be invented. There are no linguistic clues as in the case of a neurotic's free associations. A psychotic may be vaguely aware of this lack but since he or she is not engaged with the process of symbolisation in relation to the other, it is difficult, and perhaps impossible, to repair this lack. If the capacity to constantly shift from one idea or series of ideas to another and thus subtly to change meaning with each "repositioning" is not available to someone with a psychotic structure, then understanding the ever-changing motives of others becomes impossible. The psychotic is trapped in the compulsive certainty of his own reading of his fantasy—one which is unique to him in the sense that, unlike the fantasy of neurotics, it has no necessary connection, even in the indirect form of negation, with the outside world.

What then of anxiety in the world of the psychotic? There is a third register in the Lacanian canon that plays a part here—the Real. Unlike the neurotic, the psychotic cannot substitute a symptom with less painful connotations for the apprehended greater pain of the anxiety and thus create a neurotic defence. In other words, one metaphor cannot be substituted for another, since there are no metaphors available to the psychotic in the first place. Without metaphor, the constant shift from one idea to another expressed in the simplest fantasy, cannot exist. Psychotics live permanently in a world where metaphorical substitutions cannot be made. However most of us nevertheless have firsthand experience of the Real. When we are affected by trauma, a hallmark of the experience is the lack of ability to think, to remember and sometimes to feel anything at all. It is often as if time had stood still. We are now in the grip of an experience not unlike that of the psychotic. We repeat terrible experiences in nightmares, uncontrollable shivering and other deeply unpleasant symptoms. Fantasy has stopping carrying out its work. We will explore what happens to anxiety when fantasies of all kinds cease to "work" in later chapters.

Unity, negation and the role of language

As chapter one showed, most of us are "normal" neurotics; consequently, we are deeply implicated in negative dialectics not simply as a method of coping with anxiety but in order to reinforce a sense of our difference from other people. Most of us have a distinct sense of our own uniqueness, and for this reason often feel that our suffering is like that of nobody else. Yet it is a common experience of any practitioner who has to deal with human suffering that the same problems crop up again and again. Indeed, making decisions and choices in life, even if they are often inevitably incorrect ones, is a key part of dealing with the manifold problems of living. This perception of our own uniqueness is partially correct, since we construct a personal set of fantasies to fit the particular circumstances of our lives. For the same reason therefore, a *failure* to make distinctions and notice important differences can lead to a fallacious assumption of unity, distorting our relationship to the world around us. Everyone has fantasies of unity just as they have fantasies of uniqueness. For example, I might yearn to be left alone in peace to pursue my writing without interruption—nothing should be allowed to intervene or intrude. This fantasy soon breaks down however, because, in order to get to the next stage of an argument, a fresh and often provocative and disturbing idea has to be allowed to intrude on this fantasised unity of aim. The act of constructing a sustained argument necessitates interruption! New ideas take the form of language when they reach consciousness and involve a series of judgements—we have returned to the dialectical engagement with the world described in chapter one.

As well as being the stuff out of which dialectical problems and fantasies are created, language plays a key role in establishing fundamental differences in the engagement of groups of people in relation to the world in general and people in particular. In order to explain and expand this statement, we need to return to the fundamental concept of fantasy. Fantasy involves speaking and/or thinking at least partially in words. Images on their own do not tell a story unless we consciously or unconsciously supply the links. Language has multiple functions; it can be a quasi-mechanical means of communicating information from one person to another; it can be a means of distracting or diverting our thoughts from practical bodily needs such as eating, sleeping and having sex; it may be poetry. Most of these activities require the brain to function as a mind, generating flexible, sometimes unpredictable and only partially conscious responses to the world around us. Without language, we could still exist in a similar way to our cousins the chimpanzees. Without language, in today's world of competing civilizations and infinitely complex symbolic structures of communication we would live in a state of perpetual confusion.

There is another piece to fit into the jigsaw. Sexuality is partially expressed through language. Its effects both form and inhabit the structures of human thought. As Benton and Craib put it, "For Lacan the way in which we escape this extreme form of confusion is through the fixing of our desires, which primarily occurs through the development of sexuality as described by Freud." (2001, p. 164). A simple example is the difference in the sexual implications of language between that of young children and that of adults. What happens before we can speak? Even at this stage, human beings can make distinctions. For example, it has been shown that in the foetal state, infants (the Latin word "infans" means those who are without speech) have a sense of the boundaries of their own bodies and thus a sense of being "me" and "not-me" to use Winnicott's terminology (Winnicott, 1962, p. 57). As Piontelli observes, twins *in utero* suck their own thumbs—they do not suck each other's (Piontelli, 1992, p. 133). One of the parents in her study makes the following vivid series of comments about his twins' behaviour during an ultrasound examination:

"I am quite convinced that they know there is another person in there . . . that they feel boundaries . . . and have a sense of being themselves . . . but other people perhaps could argue that she is not aware that his movement comes from outside herself . . . or perhaps that they are too self-centred and absorbed to realize the existence of something and someone outside themselves . . . though these images are pretty convincing . . ." Later he added, "Of course I cannot prove it . . . but they seem to be to me to be already two very separate beings . . . each with its own clear identity." (Piontelli, 1992, p. 134)

Thus even before birth we inhabit a world with *other* people, *other* things and *other* places in it apart from the space we take up with our own bodies and on this evidence, differentiation starts in the womb. "Otherness" necessarily starts with making a distinction between two or more states. At the same time it enables most of us, through our desiring, to take up a place and "fix" ourselves in the world.

Returning to the question of language, how do we build up these distinctions in meaning? The most obvious difference is that expressed by words themselves. In English the words "hall" and "vestibule" can mean approximately the same thing—an entrance space. However, we would not refer to the famous concert hall in South Kensington named after Queen Victoria's dead consort as "The Albert Vestibule". We would of course use the word "hall" since we are referring to a large public space, not an entrance room where you leave your coat. These days, using the word "vestibule" has connotations of middle class affectation. There is a further personal meaning to the word "hall"—it is my surname. In my case, the only *absolutely fixed* meaning of "hall" is when it is used (in conjunction with my first name) to distinguish me from other people. These kinds of distinctions take place in the register that Lacan describes as imaginary.

The clearest example I have come across is found neither in psychoanalytic writing nor in the field of linguistics, but in a play entitled *Blue Heart*, by Caryl Churchill. The storyline of the Second Act is as follows: a man meets an older woman and tells her that he is the long lost baby whom she gave up for adoption. The same scenario is repeated in the play several times and each time the woman (a different character) reacts anew, with relief, with anger, with deep scepticism and so on. Roughly twenty minutes after the start of the act, one of the actors says the word "kettle" out of context but as a substitute for a word in the sentence, as if I were to write, "I kettle we are talking about the meaning of language". A couple of minutes later the same thing happens with the word "blue". Thus, "I kettle we are talking about the blue of language". At this point until the end of the play, there is a gradual but ever increasing use of the words "blue" and "kettle" and their derivatives "ble" and "ket" until hardly any other words are used. "You ble ket exactly what I'm ket, ble?" However, since the structure has been put in place, the audience in one sense has a very accurate understanding of the meaning of the interchanges on stage. At another level, what the audience is hearing is, of course, gibberish. Here we have enacted an account of how structure—unconscious structure, indeed, Lacan's "structure of the unconscious"—is required to enable language to acquire meaning. The play illustrates the existence and characteristic action of what Lacan terms "the symbolic". The dialogue takes place with an implicit understanding generated by the actors and the audience that meaning is generated by an unspoken third agency. In Lacanian terms, this agency is not symbolised as such; it takes place in a constant unconscious triangulation of terms (here two actors in a dialogue with "the other" that provides meaning) that is characteristic of the register of Lacan's Symbolic.

The above may seem a diversion from the issue of dialectics and fantasy. However, this chapter has attempted to clarify why those with a perverse and a psychotic structure think differently from those with a neurotic structure. I suggest that the clues to these differences lie in the properties of language that are explored here. Those with a psychotic structure would make nothing of Caryl Churchill's play. Similarly, someone who thinks in perverse terms might understand what is going on but be uninterested in what the play communicates—the thoughts and activities of the other are not relevant to his view of the world. Having established the involvement of language in how we arrive at thinking and indeed fantasising, we are now in a position to move and explore the interaction of anxiety with fantasy in the next chapter.

CHAPTER THREE

Working without a safety net

Fiona comes to analysis with a problem. She says, "I'm depressed and lonely, I can't have close relationships. I don't know why— my friends are all starting to live in couples, not communes and I've been left out." Fiona is now twenty-eight years old and living alone in a flat in a seedy part of town. For the last few years, she has subscribed to the alternative lifestyle offered by living on the dole and squatting. Now however, she has used her degree obtained seven years before, to go back into higher education and obtain a high-level technical qualification in the computing field.

In the first session when the analyst Fred enquires about her background, Fiona's rather monotonous and flat tone of voice suddenly changes, "I don't want to talk about my mother" she says vehemently, "It's not a safe thing to do". Fiona has a very close and protective relationship with her mother Florence who is old and frail but it is indeed only many months later that Fiona finds she is able to talk to Fred about her after all.

Fiona's father Fergal has not been seen by anyone in the family for the last twenty-five years. Fiona has never been told the reasons why her father left when she was three; her aunts and uncles and her mother Florence, all refuse to tell her. Florence and Fiona lived together on their own. Then, when Fiona was six years old, Francisco and his son Florian moved in and lived with them and some happy years of family life followed. However, eight years later, whilst Fiona was away on a school trip during the summer holidays, Francisco and Florian moved

44

out again without explanation and without saying goodbye. Once again her family refused to discuss what has happened, although this time it was evident to Fiona that Francisco was no longer getting on very well with her mother. Fiona has not seen either Francisco or Florian since. Fiona stayed at home with her mother until she left to go to university in London. Since her university days, she has either lived in squats or on her own in dingy one-bedroom flats.

Soon after her analysis starts, Fiona obtains the first of a series of good jobs and becomes very successful at work. She still feels lonely and isolated however and spends innumerable sessions in analysis pondering her fate. During this period, Fiona tracks down her father by contacting a distant relative, Fabien. She travels to Ireland to meet her father Fergal whom she finds is now suffering from Alzheimer's disease and who only just recognises her. Fiona has only one faint early memory of her father—when she fell off the swing in the park and was taken to hospital with a broken arm by her mother. She thinks her father was in the park but didn't come to the hospital, but she doesn't know whether this memory is in fact true, or if it is true, why her father didn't come to the hospital too.

As well as the sudden extremely upsetting disappearances of important people in her life, there turns out to be another reason why Fiona continues to come to analysis—the absence of any long-term sexual relationships.

We will refer to this illustration throughout this chapter and at the end, sketch out the ways in which Fred and Fiona might tackle problems of this kind.

The origins of anxiety

Psychoanalysts of differing theoretical persuasions agree on very little: however the vast majority take the view that anxiety arrives very early in the life of a human being. The situation is further complicated by the fact that there is good evidence that both the subject and object of anxiety are just as often unconscious as conscious. Finding the causes of anxiety is therefore a far from simple matter. Melanie Klein, one of the most well-known names in British psychoanalysis, describes this problem very accurately. In her paper entitled "Early Stages of the Oedipus Conflict", she has this to say:

> One of the most bitter grievances which we come upon in the unconscious is that . . . many overwhelming *questions* which are apparently only partly conscious and even when conscious cannot yet be expressed in words, remain unanswered. Another reproach follows hard upon this, namely, that the child could not understand words and speech. Thus his first questions go back beyond the beginnings of his understanding of speech.
>
> In analysis both these grievances give rise to an extraordinary amount of hate. Singly or in conjunction they are the cause of numerous inhibitions of the epistemophilic impulse: for instance, the incapacity to learn foreign languages, and, further, hatred of those who speak a different tongue. . . .
>
> The early feeling of *not knowing* has manifold connections. It unites with the feeling of being incapable, impotent, which soon results from the Oedipus situation. The child also feels this frustration the more acutely because he *knows nothing* definite about sexual processes. (Klein, 1928, p. 188 first italics mine, later italics in the original)

This passage summarises many effects of anxiety—unanswered questions, hatred of the differences exposed by questioning and the unpleasant feeling of not knowing or understanding the sexual implications of questions.

We shall start with Klein's phrase, "many overwhelming *questions* which are apparently only partly conscious and even when conscious cannot yet be expressed in words, remain unanswered". Perhaps Klein would not have generalised the problem of being human as being the problem of the place of questions. She is, I think, much more preoccupied with supplying answers in the hope that the nagging pain of the questions will go away. Klein criticised her contemporary, Anna Freud, for her view that the child must be educated in the ways of psychoanalysis before they can be analysed, basing her criticism on her own clinical experience. In her clinical practice Klein supplied interpretations offering sexual knowledge—

and answers imply the existence of questions. Here is a quotation from her analysis of a patient whom she referred to as "Dick":

> I took a big train and put it beside a smaller one and called them "Daddy-train" and "Dick-train". Thereupon he picked up the train I called "Dick" and made it roll to the window and said "Station". I explained: "The station is mummy; Dick is going into mummy." (Klein, 1930, p. 225)

This interpretation has the effect of covering over the child's ignorance with a "patch" of pre-determined "sexual knowledge". This tactic closes down the potential for open-ended questions and the ongoing pursuit of knowledge. It does not follow that offering answers (presented as certainties) necessarily reduces anxiety. I accept here that Melanie Klein has grasped at least two important points. The first is that she understands that knowledge/knowing and lack of knowledge/not knowing play a key part in the problems of the patient. The second point is a tangential but important one. Nowadays, Dick would probably be diagnosed as autistic and in terms of my argument in the previous chapter quite possibly psychotic. If this was the case, then to supply him with knowledge may be both a safe and effective course of action. However for the majority of patients who have neurotic problems, a more applicable clinical approach would be to encourage *questions*, as opposed to descriptions and answers, about the problems for children (and adults) raised by knowledge/knowing and lack of knowledge/not knowing. Questioning opens up the possibility of dialectical engagement and therefore a route to relieving the patient's anxiety. In Fiona's case, Fred can take a more flexible and effective stance if he does not rush to provide answers.

In favour of her argument, however, Melanie Klein does indicate that the role of questions is important from the beginning of life. A child wants to know who they are and about their relationship to their family. Such questions are often vital in terms of the psychic life of a person; they can also appear to be mysteriously nebulous. In particular they are about intangible and apparently unknowable questions—where babies come from is not obvious to the young child. Such questions often haunt adults too.

How do we approach the intangible and the unknowable in Fiona's story? (*I don't want to talk about my mother*). Before we can discuss anxiety in detail, it is helpful to pick up the theme of words from the end of the last chapter and investigate a different aspect of the part language plays in human life. Freud started with the words people use, particularly words which, in various ways, are at the very edge of consciousness. In Freud's view dreams and jokes both involve a use of language where, if they are to succeed, there is a disguise or distortion of the apparent—"manifest"—meaning of the words themselves. Indeed Freud wrote a whole book, *The Psychopathology of Everyday Life*, exploring Freudian slips where people say one thing but mean something else. The unconscious briefly evades repression to be spotted by the careful listener before disappearing from view again. This is the point in time, whether dream, joke or Freudian slip, when a fantasy is glimpsed. Freud took the view that words disappeared or were distorted into different meanings whenever anxiety hovered into view. Mostly people are unaware, unconscious of this process. Nevertheless, consciousness retains some clues to this phenomenon in terms of the distortions. Thus Fiona's comment that she does not want to talk suggests to Fred that there is very probably a huge amount of anxiety connected to the forbidden topic.

A common battleground between fantasy and anxiety is the activity of dreaming. *The Interpretation of Dreams* is a key early work by Freud where he puts forward his initial ideas about the nature of this battleground where anxious thoughts are changed into something altogether less troubling—it's only a dream. In the process he describes how fantasies are constructed to provide the "building blocks" of dreams. The whole book could be read as an extended essay on the idea that not only do we not know what we really think —we do not even dream what we imagine we are dreaming! Freud concludes that dreams have a meaning—precisely that which we would rather *not* know about. Thus, each of us considers that the "real meaning" of our dreams is too difficult to tangle with and that part of the process of dreaming is to conceal their true import. Freud's phrase, "dream work", sums it up—an enormous amount of effort goes into concealing ourselves from ourselves. Nevertheless, despite all the subterfuge, something is revealed in dreams and people have always recognised this. The famous story of Joseph in the Bible centred on the importance of his dreams. What is remarkable about the story is his fearless courage in following what he perceives to be the true meaning of his dreams. Why do many of us often find knowledge about our dreams so upsetting? Why don't more of us behave like Joseph? Why don't we want to know about the repressed? In Freud's early work, we find his theory of false connections where Freud theorises a breakdown in our capacity to both ask and answer questions—Fiona's dilemma.

It appears in the form of an extended footnote in the chapter about Emmy von N. in *Studies in Hysteria*:

> In place of her doubts about the lift, she informed me that she had been afraid that her period was going to start again and would again interfere with the massage. (Breuer & Freud, 1895d, p. 67)
>
> The sequence of events had accordingly been as follows: When she [Emmy] woke up in the morning she found herself in an anxious mood, and to account for it she grasped at the first anxious idea that came to mind. On the previous afternoon she had had a conversation about the lift at the Pension. Over-careful of her children as usual, she had asked their governess whether her elder daughter, who could not walk much on account of ovarian neuralgia on the right side and pains in the right leg, used the lift for going down as well as up. A paramnesia then enabled her to link the anxiety she was conscious of with the idea of the lift. Her consciousness did not present her with the real cause of her anxiety; that only emerged—but now it did so without any hesitation—when I questioned her about it in hypnosis. (p. 67)

Then

> In cases in which the true causation evades conscious perception one does not hesitate to attempt to make another connection, which one believes, although it is false. It is clear that a split in the content of consciousness must greatly facilitate the occurrence of "false connections" of this kind. (p. 67)

Here Freud is already pointing out that the ego is always fragmented. As small children, we inevitably find the world a frightening and puzzling place. Rather than remaining baffled, we will link together ideas in order to patch up this incoherent mess in an attempt to make the world meaningful. Such links are termed by Freud "false connections". As the case of Emmy von N. shows, we carry on doing so as adults.

Fiona's false connections are linked to the painful experiences of her childhood. She believes that disappearance is connected to speaking. "Keep quiet and people may stay around" and "don't attempt a long-term relationship because people always leave without telling you." Fiona's understandable response is therefore to act pre-emptively. "Make sure that you dispose of a lover before they show any inclination to stay around. That way you won't be caught out by their sudden disappearance. I'd rather *they* cried, not *me*." However, there are further implications to false connections. In spite of everything, Fiona finds herself looking for her father, in the face of the refusal of her family to help her and their collective silence on the issue. Fiona, like Julie in chapter one, is caught in a complicated web of contradictory unconscious impulses.

What is the link, if any, between a free association and false connection? Freud's answer is that free associations have links in the way words are put together, homophones, slips of the tongue, slips of the pen and so. A false connection may be indicated when the analysand provides a link during associations that seems odd, out of place, bizarre even, and yet the analysand is convinced of its obvious often self-evident truth. An analyst knows that they have stumbled upon a false connection when the analysand, in response to an interpretation, says something like "what a stupid remark"! (I am being polite here) At this point, it is a reasonable bet that they are trying to throw the analyst off the scent.

Staying with the familiar, with what we know, avoiding change trapped in the same old repetitions, habits and rituals expressed in the symptom is our universal attempt to maintain the illusion of unity, sameness—the baby's reluctance to give up the fantasised unity with mother is only the first of many subsequent reluctances. All revolutions are difficult and dangerous. Psychoanalysis *is* the stuff of dreams. Thus Fred has to find ways to encourage Fiona to put into words ideas that she finds too terrifying at present even to contemplate. Gradually she will be encourage to produce ideas that she may feel are in contradiction with her symptoms. It is not only the attempt to render some small aspects of the unacceptable unconscious, conscious; it is also allowing people to dream more freely. Is this the direction of anarchy?

People have various tactics at their disposal in their attempt to maintain the *status quo*. For example, they often use particular words or phrases as leitmotifs for their lived experience, as meaningless fillers to patch over spaces in their discourse which, if left open, might allow more painful thoughts which are different, divisible, evanescent and fleeting to appear. Examples of words or phrases that function in this way are "blah, blah, blah", "stuff". Tony Blair's version is "yu'see".

This introductory linking of fantasy and anxiety places language at the centre of our thinking. Experiences in life that are beyond words are described by Freud as "the uncanny" and Lacan as "the Real"; this is where our story leads to next.

The uncanny

Trying to avoid anxiety by dodging awkward questions and uncomfortable answers does not always work. At best, this tactic results in a partial solution. What happens when the experience of anxiety overwhelms everything else including our capacity to pretend, via dreams, jokes or Freudian slips that things are not really as they seem? Freud wrote a paper on this topic called "The Uncanny" (Freud, 1919h). In the original German, the phrase Freud uses is "*Das Unheimliche*". As Freud tells us in his paper, "*Heim*" in German is the word for "home". Thus, when we have the experience of something being so frightening that we do not want to know what it is, then we are having the experience of something *at home within* us being so frightening that we either do not or perhaps more accurately cannot put a name to it. We eject it from our thoughts, trying to put it "outside" ourselves. Anxiety of this kind is something we cannot name and that appears to have no shape or form. Its effects can seem contradictory since anxiety is often experienced as something "out there—a stranger to us". At the same time, it emanates from within us.

Putting this in more concrete terms, Freud argues that when we are frightened of something—snakes, the dark, horses and so on— this is fear, something qualitatively different from anxiety. The latter is infinitely more terrifying precisely because we *can't* identify the source of our fears. When Freud discusses the uncanny, he uses a literary rather than a clinical source, *The Sand-Man*, a famous short story by E. T. A. Hoffman. The tale is perhaps more familiar in the guise of the first act of Offenbach's *Tales of Hoffmann* or Delibe's ballet *Coppelia*. The story focuses on eyes. Nathaniel, the central character of the story, is threatened by his mother that the Sand-Man:

> ... [T]hrows handfuls of sand thrown into his eyes so that they jump out of their heads all bleeding. Then he puts the eyes in a sack and carries them off to the half-moon to feed his children. They sit up there in their nest, and their beaks are hooked like owls' beaks, and they use them to peck up naughty boys' and girls' eyes with. (Freud, 1919h, p. 228)

Later in the story, Nathaniel falls in love with Olympia and only belatedly, and after much denial, realises that she is simply a puppet—she can't *really* see or feel anything. The story is a subtle and confusing blend of different varieties of fantasy; the distinctions between the "reality" of the story and Nathaniel's hallucinations become increasingly hard to detect until eventually the reader realises that Nathaniel has been driven mad. The trauma caused by the visits of the Sand-Man is the pivotal link in the plot. As Freud succinctly puts it, "... the feeling of something uncanny is directly attached to the figure of the Sand-Man, that is, to the idea of being robbed of one's eyes and ... an intellectual uncertainty has nothing to do with the effect" (Freud, 1919h, p. 230). As in Fiona's case, we can see via the repetition of events in the story that each approaches the dread of losing ones eyes in a different way. We can also see the dilemma that acute anxiety brings—shall we remain like rabbits, paralysed by fear when caught in the headlights of a car, or shall we act and court the possibility of worse problems? *Shall I talk about my mother?—or shall I stay with the familiarity of my anxiety and keep silent?*

Freud claims that anxiety and its effects are linked to trauma, the state of mind we experience when something is so awful that we cannot remember it but find ourselves constantly "reliving" the experience in nightmares, sweating, or apparently unreasoning terrors. Freud's shorthand for these experiences is "the repetition compulsion". Thus, a recurrent theme in many analyses is the role of trauma—in Fiona's case—the long-term effects of sudden un-announced and unexplained disappearances and their habit of repeating their effects in later life via mechanisms such as projection and transference.

So far we have established that anxiety is differentiated from fear. If it does not have an obvious object, nevertheless it is implicated in both effects and affects. Even more puzzlingly, it can seem as if anxiety has no subject either. Fiona does not want to talk about the object of her anxiety—in this case possibly her mother; nor does she want to talk about the "subject", i.e. herself in relation to either her mother or the anxiety. She has no words to describe either state. Yet it is clear that Fiona experiences her suffering as result of *something*. So how can we connect this strange absence to something tangible or audible? Freud's observations concerning the uncanny being "at home" and "out of sight, out of mind" at one and the same time hove into view again.

How can we characterise the "void" that results from our experi-ence of the uncanny? Freud argues that this "void" does not have an object but there is a clear example of transference when Nathaniel identifies a lawyer, Coppelius, who occasionally comes to dinner, with his early fear of the Sand-Man. Something is identified in this story as moving, precipitating an emotion, causing an effect.

Interestingly at the end of his paper, Freud veers away from the disturbing nature of his own conclusions. On the one hand he says:

> . . . [A]n uncanny effect is often and easily produced when the distinction between imagination and reality is effaced, as when something that we have hitherto regarded as imaginary appears before us in reality, or when a symbol takes over the full functions of the thing it symbolizes, and so on. . . . [T]he infantile element in this, which also dominates the minds of neurotics, is the over-accentuation of psychical reality in comparison with material reality—a feature closely allied to the belief in the omnipotence of thoughts. (Freud, 1919h, p. 244)

Yet, two pages later, we find the following:

Fairy tales quite frankly adopt the animistic standpoint of the omnipotence of thoughts and wishes, and yet I cannot think of any genuine fairy story which has anything uncanny about it. Freud, 1919h, p. 246)

Freud has conveniently forgotten the terrifying original versions of stories such as Little Red Riding Hood. In one early rendering by Perrault, she is eaten up and the moral of the tale is, "talk to strangers at your peril"; in others she unwittingly eats her grandmother's flesh and blood before escaping from the wolf. The belief in the "omnipotence of thoughts" to which he refers is rather the child's often unsuccessful attempt to escape the predations of the uncanny, not a generally harmless substitute.

The real

The debate about the disturbing and mysterious nature of Freud's uncanny is taken further in the Lacanian concepts of the "the Real" and the "object *a*" discussed in detail in his unpublished seminar *L'Angoisse* (Anxiety). Lacan's occasionally obscure writing style mirrors the subtle, often fleeting states of mind which leave barely detectable effects in consciousness but at the same time may be crucial determinants in our unconscious life.

The Real is a difficult concept to grasp. In some sense, it describes something that lacks, is wanting. It ignores or perhaps even does away with differences and discrimination. Just as Freud observed that the unconscious is in some senses timeless, Lacan observes that there is an aspect of the unconscious that does away with the perception of difference. Roberto Harari's excellent *Lacan's Seminar on "Anxiety": an Introduction* illustrates this point clearly:

Structurally speaking anxiety—Real—suspends the functioning of the imaginary mapping that intuitively recognises the difference between an inside and an outside ... Lacan focuses on the necessity for preserving lack—unlike what a good many official analysts maintain with their efforts to make analysands "accept lack" in the sense of accepting "realistic" limitations. (Harari, 2001, pp. 162–3)

Lacan offers a vivid definition of the Real in *Seminar II*:

> [T]here's an anxiety-provoking apparition of an image which summarises what we can call the revelation of that which is least penetrable in the real, of the real lacking any possible mediation, of the ultimate real, of the essential object which isn't an object any longer, but this something faced with which all words cease and all categories fail, the object of anxiety *par excellence*. (Lacan, 1988 [1954–55], p. 164)

This quotation encapsulates some of the qualities of anxiety; terror, bafflement, wordless emotion and a lingering feeling that there is still something there . . . and if there *is* something there, it produces a variety of effects, characterised by Lacan as the objet *a*.

Later, in *Seminar X*, Lacan suggests that anxiety, contrary to Freud's view, *does* have objects. He links these to the partial objects identified by Freud, in *The Three Essays on Sexuality*, the breast, the faeces and the phallus. Lacan adds the gaze and the voice to this list. Each of these "species" of objet *a* produces a phanteme, a building block of unconscious fantasy. Throughout Lacan's account of anxiety is the perception that, even in anxiety states where someone seems paralysed by terror, the psyche is actually still on the move, often oscillating between one intolerable idea and another and reduced to a strange phenomenon, a maelstrom of intensely disturbing and conflicting ideas which produce—motionlessness! Freud's account of the uncanny suggests a void, an absence. Lacan introduces motion into the equation, but in a very particular sense.

Indeed, unlike some analysts, Lacan emphasises the necessity for preserving lack, the feelings of aloneness, desolation or yearning so that we can continue to keep moving. We need the constant sensation that there is something for us to move into, towards, away from, something that will keep us from being static. The use of questioning as a feature of analysis enables the analysand to shift from being immobilised by anxiety to being capable of gradual shifts (movements) in perception of what it is that causes their suffering. Questions in themselves also act as a prompting to movement. They require a search for an answer. We have now hinted at the role of trauma, movement (and thereby time) into the complex story of fantasy and its relationship to anxiety. Following the earlier quotation from Melanie Klein, we now need to add a third ingredient—sexuality.

Time, sex and trauma

Psychiatrists often use the phrase "Post Traumatic Stress Disorder" (PTSD) classified in *The Diagnostic and Statistical Manual of Mental Disorders* (latest version *DSM-IV-TR*) or *The International Statistical Classification of Diseases and Related Health Problems* (latest version, *ICD10*) to describe the suffering of victims of trauma. A cynical view of these manuals is that their primary purpose is to reduce anxiety in the mind of the psychiatrist—labelling someone as suffering from "bipolar disorder", for example, provides the comforting illusion that you have advanced your knowledge of the cause of the patient's suffering. As Chris Oakley, a colleague of mine once remarked, "Nobody has ever been cured through the use of *DSM-IV*". This label accurately encompasses the fact that sufferers have all experienced something traumatic, whether it is shellshock, a disastrous earthquake or sexual abuse. The problem with using the label in context of charting the relationship between (fantasies or indeed the lack of them) and anxiety is that the label describes only one aspect of the problem. It omits any reference to the continuing and subtle effects of sexuality and time. For these reasons we will continue this discussion using psychoanalytic arguments since they alone attempt to provide a means of dynamic understanding of the suffering produced by fantasy and anxiety, rather than a simple description of an anxiety-state or a hallucination. Fiona's dilemma will not be helped if Fred sticks a label on her problems.

Early in his career, Freud latched on to a curious fact: children who are exposed to one or more traumatic incidents often do not appear traumatised at the time. Their traumata are only experienced much later, when, as adults, some apparently unrelated incident activates a reaction producing any one or more of a variety of symptoms such as panic attacks, memory lapses, depression, anorexia and so forth. Even if an earlier event cannot be remembered consciously, some perhaps quite trivial aspect of the later one reactivates the earlier experience, this time traumatically. In his writings, Freud used the term "*Nachträglichkeit*" to describe this effect. Strachey translates *Nachträglichkeit* as "deferred action" in the Standard Edition. In their dictionary entry on the term, Laplanche and Pontalis show that Freud made frequent use of the "nachträglich" in his writings. However, it is virtually impossible to follow the sequence of his thinking in the English translation because Strachey does not translate the term consistently (Laplanche & Pontalis, 1973, p. 111). The German dictionary *Langenscheidt* gives the following definition of "nachträglich" as an adjective, "additional; supplementary; subsequent; belated" and adverbially also "with hindsight". If a trauma can produce extreme effects from a starting point of no apparent direct cause, a problem with this translation becomes evident. An uninformed reading of the phrase "deferred action" could construe it as a kind of "variable time-lapse between stimulus and response" to quote Laplanche and Pontalis. They go on to show that for Freud *nachträglich* means

- A deferred revision of unassimilated experience;
- This deferred revision is sparked off by later events or by the maturing sexuality of the person;
- In the Wolf Man case, Freud points out that the Wolf Man "only understood his parents' coitus" at the time of the dream when he was four years old, not at the time of the observation. He received the impressions when he was one and a half. (Laplanche & Pontalis, 1973, pp. 111–14)

The implication of this analysis is that for the Wolf Man's phobia to erupt, it was necessary for the view of his parents' coitus to be worked over in the dream. Therefore, there is an element of psychic activity involved—a very different concept from the passive idea of a variable time lapse. More recently, Laplanche has suggested that a more appropriate English translation of the word *Nachträglichkeit* would be "afterwardsness" (Laplanche, 1992, p. 15).

However, Laplanche has his own theoretical take on the complex relationship between the unconscious and trauma represented by *Nachträglichkeit*. He makes use of a concept he terms "the enigmatic signifier". Laplanche brings the notion of seduction to the fore. He draws attention to Freud's use of *nachträglich* in the "Knödel" (dumpling) dream in *The Interpretation of Dreams* (Freud, 1900a, pp. 204–7). He points out that Freud concentrates on the "adult man who, seeing the child at the wet-nurse's breast, retroactively (*nachträglich*) imagines all that he could have drawn erotically from that situation if only he had known." The feelings of the man and the child are accounted for, but what of those of the wet-nurse—what of her sexuality? Laplanche suggests that this is the introduction of a third term—the nurse's message to the child which he terms "the enigmatic message". The message is enigmatic because it is received, but not understood, by the child. Thus for Laplanche, *Nachträglichkeit* is not a two-directional concept relating to time. He is suggesting that it operates via a third term, in this example, the wet-nurse's sexuality which occupies the role of the enigmatic signifier.

Lacan takes up the complications concerning time in the conceptualisation of *Nachträglichkeit*, the problem of how to interpret the meaning of the time lapse, in one of his famous papers in *Écrits*, "The Function and Field of Speech and Language in Psychoanalysis":

> He [Freud] annuls the times for understanding (instant du regard) in favour of the moments for concluding (moment de conclure) which precipitate the meditation of the subject towards deciding the meaning to attach to the original event. (Lacan, 1977, p. 48)

Lacan makes use of the famous logical problem known as "the prisoner's dilemma". His formulation is clearly described in the notes to another translation by Wilden as follows, "three prisoners are shown three white and two black patches by the governor of the prison. The first prisoner to discover whether he has a white or a black patch will be granted his freedom. The prisoners are not allowed to communicate with each other." Wilden continues:

> Lacan analyzes the intersubjective process in which each man has to put himself in the place of the others and to gauge the correctness of his deductions through their actions in time, from the *instant du regard* to the *moment de conclure*. The first moment of the *temps pour comprendre* is a wait (which tells each man that no one can see two black patches), followed by a decision by each that he is white ("if I were black, one of the others would have already concluded that he is white because nobody has as yet started for the door.") Then they all set off towards the door and all hesitate in a retrospective moment

of doubt. The fact that they *all* stop sets them going again. This hesitation will only be repeated twice (in this hypothetically ideal case), before all three leave the prison cell together. (Lacan, 1968, pp. 105–6)

This whole argument about time and trauma is undeniably complex. Let us return to Fiona for a moment to clarify the question being debated here by Freud, Lacan and Laplanche. It can be summarised as follows: what is the cause of Fiona's traumatised way of dealing with the world that causes all her relationships to fail? A second and perhaps more intriguing question then follows—does using a different theory produce different interpretations and do these then affect patients either positively or negatively? Before we can investigate this question, we need to distinguish between these three theories.

Freud consistently favours the primal scene, in other words he lays emphasis on the overarching impact of the earliest experience of trauma as the causal explanation for later events in Fiona's life. In the context of anxiety, for example, he asserts, "They [repressions] presuppose the operation of earlier, *primal repressions*, which exert an attraction on the more recent situation (Freud, 1926d, p. 94)." For Freud, Fiona's problems with relationships would all stem from the earliest traumatic experience in her life, the sudden unexplained disappearance of her father. His view therefore places the emphasis on Fiona remembering events as far back in childhood as she can and Freud himself sometimes "constructed" events in the past life of his patients—for example the Wolf Man—that they could not directly remember but which Freud claimed could be inferred from material such as dreams that they brought to analysis (Freud, 1918b, pp. 37–8 ft6). Using similar reasoning, Freud comes to the conclusion in this case study that the primal scene consisted in the Wolf Man seeing his parents having sex "*a tergo*" where the man enters the woman from the rear.

Consequently, if Fred is a Freudian he will be intent on exploring the details of Fiona's earliest experiences in order to alleviate her suffering. Fred might even speculate that there is a sexual "primal scene" in the style of the Wolf Man in Fiona's past and that this primal scene is the source of her suffering.

If Fred follows Laplanche, he might focus on Fiona's problems with sexual relationships and privilege this aspect of her experience in terms of listening to her story. However Laplanche by no means exclusively emphasizes the importance of the enigmatic signifier. The life (sexual) drive and death drive are always intertwined in his writings. He uses the term "propping up" to describe how one supports the other, his variant on Freud's *Anlehnung* (contact) *Anlehnen* (to lean against).

Lacan would doubt both the Freudian and the Laplanchean explanation of Fiona's trauma. The example of the prisoners' dilemma illustrates Lacan's view that there is no single event that causes trauma. There is an original traumatic event, a waiting time during which the trauma is "understood" and finally a moment when a conclusion is drawn, often a time of another trauma. Fiona has not one instance but recurring instances of the same kind of trauma testified by the disappearance of her father Fergal followed by Francisco and his son Florian at a later date. Lacan argues that this later event does not cause the earlier event to be remembered in the sense of putting something into words, of remembering it. Indeed what is striking about trauma is the fact that people like Fiona do *not* remember things.

In practice, it is likely that Fred would not literally apply any of these three theories. Analysands bring complex stories and trauma is only one aspect of Fiona's troubled life. Equally, drawing attention to the different style of theorising in Freud, Laplanche and Lacan flags the fact that psychology often offers a description—PTSD—rather than an explanation. Psychoanalytic theories try to offer a means of understanding something of the patient's story and an individually "tailored" response to the story is the work of the analysis. Each of these theories of trauma would alert Fred to the importance of considering factors in Fiona's story such as the passage of time, the words she is able (or unable) to speak, and quite possibly he would listen attentively to Fiona's sexual fantasies—all factors ignored or irrelevant to PTSD as described in *DSM IV*.

Conclusion

This chapter will conclude with some thoughts on how Fred might try to help a patient like Fiona. Fiona is indeed in pain, partially brought about by trying to adhere to the theoretical stance of Parmenides alluded in chapter one. In the light of our discussion of negative dialectics in that chapter, we might think that in reality, at the beginning of the analysis, Fiona desperately wants to talk about her mother but finds herself unable to voice anything except a denial —but is it always correct to draw this conclusion? Two years later, Fiona herself is finally able to comment that she was terrified that the analysis, in some completely unclear and unspecified (and therefore terrifying) way, would ensure her separation from her one remaining relative. This may seem completely irrational, but terror accurately describes the mysterious nameless something that prevents people from talking about experiences that have left lasting and often indelible impressions upon them.

Fred might take the view that Fiona's early experience has resulted in an extreme form of anxiety termed trauma. Amongst other symptoms, it is characterised by an inability to speak about the original cause of the anxiety. Traumatised people like Fiona often find psychoanalysis unbearable because any questioning, however gentle, feels like aggravating a gaping and sore wound and risks bringing back horrific memories that have been carefully buried for many years. To continue with the surgical metaphor, sometimes wounds need opening and cauterising, since only then do they have a chance of healing. Psychoanalysis offers the hope, not a promise, that the experience of speaking about the previously unspeakable will enable a healing process to take place so that patients can live their lives with renewed passion, enjoyment and vigour. Some, however, find that reopening old wounds causes too much pain. They may leave analysis or spend time avoiding the areas of their experience that are too heavily tinged with trauma. As Lacan remarks in his *Seminar X* on anxiety, "After all to sense what the subject can tolerate, in terms of anxiety, is something that puts you to the test at every instant" (Lacan, 1962–63, p. 2).

The problem for both Fred the analyst and his patient Fiona is whether she is waiting for Fred to show her that there is a door she can open, or is she telling him that, for very good reasons, the door should remain firmly shut? Note that it is not the analyst's job to open the door for Fiona, since, apart from the fact that this might have a disastrous result, such an action involves putting the analyst in the ethically problematic position of presuming to know what is good for the patient. Since nobody has a degree in mind reading, how can anyone "know" what is best for someone else?

We will isolate some of the factors that might produce anxiety and the responses that people often make in such situations. We will start with a well-known psychoanalytic phenomenon that plays an essential part in the attempt to deal with traumatic anxiety—transference.

Transference is often used both wittingly and unwittingly by those in positions of power to control others or at the very least able to dispense advice—doctors, politicians and teachers to name but a few. As we noted above, at the beginning of her analysis, Fiona avoids the topic of her mother. Fiona is convinced that the way to deal with absences and losses is to remain silent. In the past, nobody ever explained to her why people she loved left, so now the idea that she should explore the absences in her life by talking about them with someone else may be both puzzling and terrifying. Fiona has learned a painful lesson very early in life, reinforced by the disappearance of her stepfather and stepbrother a few years later, "ask no questions and you get no answers" with two additional twists. If you *do* ask questions, those around you give you the message that it is too painful even to listen to the question; secondly, Fiona may have the fantasy that the questions themselves are the cause of people's departure in her life. Thus, people leave rather than wait for the question. This attitude, learned from her mother and her mother's relatives, may be "transferred" to the analyst.

Fiona's anxiety gradually fades when the analyst Fred does not disappear but is there every week, and when he refuses to put a topic out of bounds, always allowing Fiona to talk about what she wants to talk about rather than setting an agenda. Then and only then, is Fiona able to start talking about her mother, Florence. Not forcing someone to talk about something they find intolerably painful sometimes permits them the space and time to find a way to talk about the previously unspeakable. In some cases, people spend years in analysis before they can confront trauma in their lives.

One way of conceptualising Fiona's anxiety might be to consider the possibility that transference, in this case transferring her anxiety about disappearance in general, to the particular situation of her relationship with the analyst Fred, operates as a kind of safety net. However, in *Seminar X L'Angoisse*, Lacan points out that analysts have to work "without a net", since ". . . there is no net, because precisely as regards anxiety, each mesh, as I might appropriately put it, has no meaning except precisely by leaving the void in which anxiety is." (Lacan, 1962–63, p. 6) The experience of anxiety is such that if Fiona tries to talk about it she feels she will fall into . . . what?—a void?—a trap? Twisting Lacan's words somewhat, anxiety raises the stakes for the analysand, so much so, that it is like being a novice tightrope walker without a safety net. The analyst can't provide a net because any net falls into the category of making a decision about the patient's life and deciding what is best for her.

Yet, in a strange way, the transference offers people like Fiona the illusion of a safety net, an unconscious belief that difficult and dangerous emotions will be safely caught and dealt with: "This anger I feel toward all my relatives for being silent about the disappearing acts all around me need not go into free fall; it can be safely caught by the analyst Fred. He will listen to my shouts of rage and he won't disappear too." But however closely Fred listens, Fred will never experience Fiona's terror from the same perspective. Fred can't "cure" Fiona's anxiety—at best he can only help her find her own probably partial solutions to the problems in her life that cause her to suffer. For the greatest fear of someone in Fiona's situation may be that, without the safety net, she will fall into an abyss of complete loneliness. From an existential point of view, Fiona is indeed alone. When Margaret Thatcher proclaimed there is no such thing as a society, in a strict sense she is correct. However, exchanging one cliché for another, perhaps it would be more accurate to say that "no man is an island" is more accurately rendered as "each person is an island surrounded by lots of other islands".

There are two distinctly different analytic approaches to helping someone with a problem like Fiona's. One point of view is that, with the help of analysis, Fiona may gradually to come to terms with many disappointments, including the fact that there is no net, no certainties and that she is alone in the world.

Nevertheless, there are some compensations. Learning to speak to someone about the awful void, the threatening silence that surrounds her father's mysterious absence, turns out in Fiona's case to be possible and offers much relief from her crippling anxieties. Some analysts have faith that the analytic experience *does* provide a net, that it *is* able to "contain" the analysand's terror. If the analyst, Fred, takes this view of transference, then he will encourage Fiona to form a close and platonic loving attachment to the person she *imagines* him to be in the analysis. In process of "falling in love" with the analyst, the patient is gradually helped to relive the damaging experiences of early childhood by talking about them to the analyst. The analyst conceptualises his role as a container of anxiety and he is able to provide a safety net where dangerous and difficult feelings can be explored without falling into a void.

As I indicated above, other analysts, following Lacan, think that there is no net and that the patient must be helped to find their own way to work without the false "certainties" induced by using the transference to encourage falling in love. Fiona's statement, *I don't want to talk about my mother* is very interesting. She doesn't want to talk about her mother, yet at the same time she is bringing her mother into the conversation with the analyst—this is Freud's concept of negation in action. In Fiona's case, she has to find a way of being able to speak, so that she can reduce her terror from Freud's hysterical misery to common unhappiness (Freud, 1895d). The analyst has to show her that, with or without a safety net, speaking is possible. In the second, Lacanian, approach, Fiona may still fall in love with the analyst Fred but one of the tasks of analysis will be to dismantle the transference love and encourage it to disappear rather than promoting it as a route to cure.

I will give Freud the last words, "The benighted traveller may sing aloud in the dark to deny his own fears; but, for all that, he will not see an inch further beyond his nose (Freud, 1926d, p. 96)."

Whatever you may think about safety nets, there is much work to be done.

CHAPTER FOUR

What happens when the plot gets lost

Fantasies involve stories. In order to carry out the task of diminishing anxiety, fantasy needs plots that, however speciously, make sense of what threatens to be our otherwise meaningless worlds. Our response to anxiety is not solely a random knee-jerk reaction generated by our genes but partially learned at our mother's knee. It is even plausibly argued that in the womb a foetus who is played soothing music appears less "stressed" (if that is the correct word) than one who is subjected to less pleasant stimuli such as sudden loud noises, bumps and bangs. Psychoanalysis involves the uncovering of the linked and intertwined fantasies of the patient. As I have outlined previously, each patient makes different linkages between their private fantasies, but overall, there are a limited number of psychic structures that restrict the variety of plot lines. As we saw in chapter two, Freud and Lacan argue that there are only three: neurosis, psychosis and perversion, although neurosis has a variety of subplots such as hysteria, obsessional neurosis and phobia. This chapter will therefore focus on the contribution of the plot line in the construction of fantasy.

Most good stories also have a setting. Settings do not influence the action in a story but they nuance the way we understand it. Fantasies can often be at war with each other in our heads. The Second World War coincides with a period of intense conflict within the British Psychoanalytical Society. During this time, the Society went to war over key ideas relating to fantasy—even indeed, over how it should be spelled, fantasy versus phantasy. I will return to this theme later in this chapter. Transposing a plot from one period into another offers fresh insights: thus the 1996 film version of *Richard III* setting it during the Second World War added new resonances to the play that of course Shakespeare could not have anticipated.

There is another quite different story that dates from this time. At the instigation of Myra Hess and Kenneth Clark, the National Gallery hosted a series of concerts providing classical music as a welcome relief from the horrors of the Second World War. One of the most beautiful accounts of daydreaming, that experience of drifting off into a reverie, was described in a radio talk about these concerts by E. M. Forster. While he was sitting listening to the music, sometimes he dutifully attended to the harmony, the sounds of the individual instruments and the logical progress of the musical structure; at others, he wondered whether he had turned the gas off on the stove before leaving home. Yet, at the end of the concert, he returned home curiously uplifted as the result of a profound musical experience. Paradoxically however, much of the concert had passed him by while he worried about the everyday. What strikes us about this description is the fragmentation of the experience on the one hand and the sense of an overarching unity on the other. There is no doubt that he is talking about a vivid and compelling series of feelings, yet he details the way in which his mind flew hither and thither from the sublime to the trivial and at the same time was affected in an indefinable way by the beauty of the music, leaving a coherent sense of an intensely moving and valuable experience.

In more mundane circumstances, such as reading this chapter, many readers may "lose the plot". Psychologists reckon that twenty minutes is the maximum time we can concentrate on a given task but then have little to say about the significance of this fact. Often it is irrelevant, since the reader may resume the task of reading later and follow the argument without losing any essential facts. However, in Forster's case, where *does* the music go next, or why do words burbling on suddenly seem to have embarked upon an alien thread of argument?

Losing the plot has variants. In the situation described above, someone finds another path of thinking leading off in a different direction and they wander away like E. M. Forster, possibly, but not necessarily, to return to the original path later. A second variation occurs when someone becomes completely and utterly swamped by following the endless ramifications of a complicated exposition of a theory, or rather theories, that lead them in countless directions each of which divides into several subsidiary concepts . . . such that their mind is like a horse in a show jumping arena. Having obediently followed the instructions of the rider and leapt over one difficult intellectual hurdle after another, their mind refuses the next fence and they stall—unable to think. A third occasion is a situation where what we are experiencing is not something pleasurable like a concert, or potentially intriguing such as a complex theory, but an unpleasant experience such as being dressed down by an indignant customer for having ignored the long queue snaking round the bank and addressed a question directly to the teller. If the "dressing down" goes on too long—perhaps we feel it is unjustified—we may "switch off".

The above are all examples from common social experiences without any particular traumatic input. However, most, if not all of us, have had times when we could not bear the story unfolding around us. Losing the plot (in psychological terms, losing concentration) therefore, either means that the story stops for us and leaves us feeling blank or we start creating a fantasy of our own which is more congenial, more "fanciful". These disruptions sometimes have a protective value. Shifting the focus to the clinic, many patients arrive with a story that purports to describe their life experience. In many cases the details are well rehearsed, sometimes nigh on suffocatingly so. Their close personal relationships do not work; sometimes they have never worked; sometimes the relationship has broken down. Whatever the case, they are miserable.

However, in most instances, what transpires over the early months of analysis is that there is no single account of each aspect of a person's life, but many contradictory versions, each with a different plot. The patient often assumes that each of these versions is not only "true", but part of a singular, apparently uniform, truth. Many people are surprised to discover in the course of analysis that they operate with multiple and conflicting "truths". Truth therefore has a limited currency in psychoanalysis. The moments when the patient speaks the truth are in fact the times when the unconscious is unintentionally allowed a voice (as described in the previous chapter) in the guise of jokes, dreaming and Freudian slips. Even here of course, the situation is one where the patient is saying something that he or she *believes to be true*. When the analyst listens to the story often of unremitting, persistent and continuous woe and disaster, what is arresting is hearing a series of ideas that the strike the listener as possessing aspects that are curious, strange, contradictory or even fantastical. A second curious feature is the way in which certain motifs recur, both as events that repeat—such as the man with a series of short-lived relationships with women—and the repetition of words or phrases to describe apparently disparate experiences. For example, a woman may describe herself as "always *critic*ising men" and then sometime later point out that her relationship with a man has reached "a *critic*al stage". The phoneme "critic" is unconsciously reiterated by the patient. We shall return to the repetition later.

I have used the word "fantastical" deliberately because I wish to comment on the close connection between daydreaming and fantasy. The E. M. Forster daydream, the "stalling" sensation in thinking where close attention to a logical set of ideas is demanded, and a simple refusal to think, are all examples of attempts to work through experiences sequentially in line with what we consider "external reality" (in the form of other people, events, or things) expects us to do. However, our minds either produce a fantasy—setting off on another track—or they temporarily stop thinking. Note the fact that whilst language is sequential—to put it very simply "man bites dog" has a different meaning from "dog bites man"—when the plot line falters, sequential thinking and speaking stops. This kind of sequential, rationalised and joined-up fantasying resembles the conscious account of their lives that many people offer at the start of their analysis. Another consequence of a stalling or a diversion in the thinking processes is the tendency of the psyche to form a loop. Often unconsciously, internal circular arguments are set up so that people find themselves endlessly repeating a series of actions and/or a form of words; even if they find such actions repellent or irritating, they apparently are unable to prevent an endless repetition of constant apparently undesired actions. The extreme examples of this type of behaviour are found in people with compulsions such as continual washing habits or other rituals that must be completed before life can continue. Freud termed this phenomenon the repetition compulsion.

A second situation involves fantasy of a slightly different kind. I am thinking of the sensation of a constant inner conversation with ourselves, which wanders from time to time, and on occasion jibs at thinking the next thought. Sometimes we are aware of this process and, at others, we are ignorant of it. An example is the habit of going to bed at night and falling asleep ruminating over a set of problems (whether the problems in question are life changing or entirely trivial is quite irrelevant). When you wake up, you find that you have often produced a good solution, but are unaware of the process that led to the solution. This could be said to be an effect of the preconscious interacting with the unconscious in Freudian terms where it produces an account of one's life that is mainly for internal consumption and then changes it. Freud's understanding of the importance of mnemic symbols is one of the cornerstones of his theory of hysteria. The clearest account of a mnemic symbol occurs in the first of his "Five Lectures on Psychoanalysis" where he describes the series of crosses erected to commemorate the carrying of the coffin to Westminster of Queen Eleanor, the wife of one of the Plantagenet kings. (One of them is Charing Cross and the stone is still a landmark in front of the station of the same name.) He points out that hysterics behave as if the cross, a symbol of an old grief, was invested with contemporary feelings of loss. Switching his metaphor, Freud remarks that if a stream divides into two courses and one becomes blocked, then the other will overflow. In other words, the grief associated with one idea may have its avenue to consciousness blocked because that avenue is overwhelmed with emotion. It may therefore overflow into other less appropriate but nonetheless convenient paths. (Freud, 1910, pp. 16–17)

Dreams are a step further away from the influence of the external world and conscious thinking processes, although their external effects may still be very influential. The lynchpin of Freud's theory of dreams is his understanding that they provide a means of processing disturbing unconscious anxieties from the "day's residue". The diminished level of anxiety enables the dreamer to carry on sleeping. Freud's theory of dreams was considered untrue for many years, as a result of research into the different kinds of sleep experienced during the night and the finding that Rapid Eye Movement (REM) sleep is qualitatively different from deep sleep. REM sleep was thought to coincide with dreaming. However, recent research by the neuro-psychoanalyst, Mark Solms, indicates that, on the contrary, dreaming may occur during both sleeping states. Furthermore, lack of the ability to dream (perhaps caused as a result of lesions to the brain) can result in lack of motivation in life (Solms, 2000). Solms concludes his paper with the observation that research has in essence come full circle—we still do not know the biological reason for dreaming. If this is the case, the psychological reasons seem just as speculative, since much psychological research looks to biology to underpin its findings. Neither biology nor psychology answer the question: what is dreaming *for*? Diminution of anxiety still seems a possible candidate, whether or not linked to the ability to sleep. The anecdotal and empirical evidence of improved capacity to think through problems after dreaming also point in this direction.

Thus far, we have a series of conscious and semi-conscious fantasies internally generated in response to anxiety. There is a further related series of fantasies embodied in the dream. The world around us is populated with fantasy constructions in the form of film, TV programmes, books, computer games and the like; these will be considered in the next chapter. I now wish to add a fourth kind of fantasy, those unconscious fantasies that operate in the drive. Many psychoanalysts have commented on Freud's use of the term "*Triebe*" and the misleading nature of its translation into English as "instincts". Drives are not usually directly accessible to consciousness but, nonetheless, there is good evidence for their existence. They are the fantasies that operate in situations where people "act out". This can be dramatic. A psychiatric in-patient may smash a window because they cannot put their angry thoughts into words. They "smash" through their unspeakably aggressive feelings and simply "go straight for jugular". It can also be ordinary. What is the insistence that "drives" students to write their essays at the last minute when they have had three months to prepare?

The account of fantasy put forward so far suggests that although there may be a structure to fantasy, it is very complex. It explains the doubt of the analyst when confronted for the first time with a new patient. Is the patient's version of their life really the whole truth—is this *really* the story? —is there *more* to the story? —and so on. It is my contention that we all have a series of fantasies that operate in the modes described above. These fantasies are piled up in a kind of logjam. Pursuing this metaphor further, we can think of a group of beavers, which carefully manoeuvre logs into position to make a dam in order to raise the level of a river without completely obstructing the flow of water. The dam functions as an analogy for the structure of repression as the neurotic's means of stemming the flow of anxiety. If someone cannot bear one or more aspect of their love relationships, they do not content themselves with one fantasy. They construct a series of different fantasies, each consisting of a different log. Many logs will be "positioned" in such a way that apparently they cannot be disturbed. The logs sometimes are positioned to keep diametrically opposed views separate and exert an equal and opposite force upon each other. Sometimes the dam can also function as analogy for the structure of psychosis, when the logs are forced together in an attempt at fusion. On yet other occasions, the logs will exert force in the same direction, the sheer weight of the wood preventing the water from flowing with its full force. Beavers spend their time not only building but rebuilding dams, an inherently repetitive activity. The collective function of both similar and contradictory fantasies is, therefore, an intricate structure which uses the same materials but produces a unique tailor-made "dam" in each individual, their own personalised response to both welcoming and fending off external reality.

To return to the psychoanalytic process, how can a psychoanalyst intervene in a situation where reality is a relative term and where not one but several different kinds of fantasying are in operation? As ever, it is helpful to start with the patient. Sooner or later, the average hysteric will say something along the lines, "my life is miserable, my relationships are a mess" and to quote Mrs. Thatcher, "there is no alternative"—TINA for short. TINA is presented as a unitary whole, in spite of the many variants to the individual's misery. One classic analytical intervention consists of a simple question: why? The effect of such an intervention is to interpolate a note of questioning or doubt into the apparently unified and uniform wall of misery represented by TINA.

For the analyst therefore, it follows that a third task in analysing fantasy is not only to disrupt fantasies which lead to painful and often stupefyingly boring circular closed arguments, but to expose the way in which the fantasies we construct are connected to each other. The work is not directional since, at times, the analyst tries to enable the patient to prise apart apparently fused fantasies and at others to enable the patient to connect aspects of his or her life that have been rigidly separated. In this way, the patient can be freed to think about the function of such connections and the relationship of the connection to their symptoms.

This is a view of fantasy as a discordant and disrupted narrative where only the superficial appearance of the structure has a sequential and logical narrative. In reality we all, patients and analysts alike, spend much of our lives constructing constantly changing and at the same time repetitive narratives to paper over the cracks of our flawed thinking and the consequent sudden outbreaks of anxiety. We produce endlessly inventive accounts of our existence "after the event". Tall stories, taking an account of bravery with a pinch of salt, and picking out the odd nugget of truth concealed in a political manifesto are all evidence that human beings in some sense are aware of their endless capacity for lying, or should we be kinder and term it "fantasying" or "mythmaking"? Beavers' work is never done . . .

Returning to the setting of The Second World War, during the Controversial Discussions, the Kleinians produced, in effect, a political manifesto for fantasy. The name of the paper, which has Susan Isaacs' name on the by-line, is "The Nature and Function of Phantasy" (Isaacs, S., 1952). The view of fantasy presented in this paper displays an all-embracing vocabulary; for example, "All impulses, all feeling, all modes of defence are experienced in phantasies which give them *mental* life and show their direction and purpose." (Isaacs, S., 1952: p. 83) In effect, this paper claims that the unconscious *is* phantasy; Isaacs makes a distinction, presumed by the Kleinians to be important, between conscious and unconscious fantasy, spelling the latter with a "ph". Doubtless, there are unconscious fantasies, but are they different in kind and structure from the conscious version? How would we "measure" the difference? Whilst this view conforms to the sheer weight of the logs in the beaver analogy, such quotations offer no opportunity for discriminating between one kind of fantasy and another. The distinction between unconscious, preconscious and conscious that is present in the early pages of Freud is elided. The Freudian distinction has the advantage, discussed in chapter one, that it opens the door for the analysis of difference in contradistinction to the analysis of similarity. A fundamental difference that human beings have to negotiate is the difference between aliveness and deadness and its corollary, the distinction between fantasy and reality. Here is Isaacs' view on this topic:

In their developed forms, phantasy-thinking and reality-thinking are distinct mental processes, different modes of obtaining satisfaction. The fact that they have a distinct character when fully developed, however, does not necessarily imply that reality-thinking *operates* quite independently of unconscious phantasy. It is not merely that they "blend and interweave"; their relationship is something less adventitious than this. In our view, *reality-thinking cannot operate without concurrent and supporting unconscious phantasies*; e.g. we continue to "take things in" with our ears, to "devour" with our eyes, to "read, mark, learn and inwardly digest", throughout life. (Isaacs, 1952, pp. 108–9)

This is an interesting passage since it conceals an inherent logical problem. On the one hand, phantasy-thinking and reality-thinking are defined as distinct mental processes. On the other, they are not simply deemed to "blend and interweave", but in addition, "reality-thinking cannot operate without concurrent and supporting unconscious phantasies". If the two are conflated, then how can we know whether anything is "real" since it always, on this account, possesses an unquantifiable admixture of "phantasy"? Furthermore, this account offers no means of distinguishing one fantasy from another; it presupposes that all fantasies have the same function (a point of view implied in the singular, unifying theme of the title of the paper). To return to the beaver analogy, the concept of a complex individualised structure, beyond the simple admixing of "reality-thinking" and "unconscious phantasies", is missing. The paper tells us there is a dam but nothing about the structure of the dam—how much is above the water level and visible (conscious) and how much is invisible (unconscious)—are the logs criss-crossed, laid in the same direction or interwoven and so on?

I think I have quoted sufficiently from Susan Isaacs' paper to demonstrate that the Kleinian version of fantasy will not do. The concept becomes so generalised in her hands that consequently it offers no theoretical potential as a meaningful clinical conceptualisation. The theory is in itself a demonstration of the tendency to fusion in human thinking. Isaacs' theory may be comforting in its simplicity, but not necessarily true. The effect of reducing the chances of difference or variation results in an increased feeling of certainty and a concomitant reduction in anxiety. The possibility of any incursion into the wall of certainty must be constantly defended against. There are no chinks in this armour. Another view is that a monolithic account of fantasy leaves no room for weaving a story.

* * *

There are more varied and nuanced accounts of the phenomenon of fantasy in a clinical context and we will turn next, not to a psychoanalyst, but to the work of the well-known anthropologist, Claude Lévi-Strauss. Lévi-Strauss makes much use of the dialectical and differentiating possibility of the story line as encapsulated in myths. I wish to look at some aspects of his paper entitled "The Structural Study of Myth" in *Structural Anthropology* (Lévi-Strauss, 1963). In some cases I have used my own translation of the French version of this paper because of the many infelicities of the English translation, not least, the use of the word "denial" to translate "négation". Lévi-Strauss revolutionised anthropology by arguing that it was essential to look for underlying unconscious structures in societies. One of the many consequences of this argument is his demonstration of the important role of myths for the organisation and functioning such structures. This, of course, is a very Freudian idea. As Paul Verhaeghe has pointed out, Freud made extensive use of myths, including Oedipus and Narcissus; when he was unable to find one he thought suitable, he devised one of his own making, a "home-made myth" such as the myth of the killing of the Primal Father in *Totem and Taboo* (Verhaeghe, 1999, pp. 198 and 200).

There is an interesting relationship between myth and fantasy; the two words are not entirely synonymous. They embody two separate but closely related ideas. The first is that a myth functions like a dream for a group, in the sense that, whereas individuals make use of dreams to ward off individual anxieties, a myth is a group fantasy that is used to ward off the collective anxieties of the group. This is an individual versus group phenomenon and focuses on the similarity between dream and myth. A second and equally interesting consideration is that there is a difference in the *structure* of a myth that separates it and distinguishes it from the *structure* of a dream. If the function of dreams and myths were identical then why would we so frequently find both in human culture? Many mammals dream, but they do not construct myths. Mammals cannot use language to communicate in the subtle and manifold ways open to humans. Myths enable the contents and anxiety-reducing function of individual dreams to be made available to the group—hence the importance of shamanism in many cultures. For the same reason TV has an insatiable demand for myths (new storylines) to fill their schedules.

What are the similarities in structure between myth and dream? Both often have storylines that reflect Oedipal conflict. According to Freudian theory, one of the key reasons for such conflict is the constant tension between the wish to see ourselves as the centre of our own individual universe and the external restrictions placed upon us by existence. To put it in an extreme sense, we may wish to be omnipotent—as Freud puts it, "his majesty the baby". The reality of adult, let alone infantile, life is that we are dependent upon others, we are each a tiny cog in the larger workings of the culture we belong to and, if we are honest, then we are mere specks in the life of the universe at large. The dissolution of the Oedipus complex is the result of each individual's struggle with these conflicting demands. The myth of the Oedipus complex can be read therefore as our attempts to negotiate the insults to our narcissism posed by the experience of growing up in any society. I shall let Lévi-Strauss take up the story from here in his own words:

> There is a very good reason why myth cannot simply be treated as language if its specific problems are to be solved; myth is language: to be known, myth has to be told; it is a part of human speech. In order to preserve its specificity we must be able to show that it is both the same thing as language, and also something different from it. Here, too, the past experience of linguists may help us. For language itself can be analyzed into things, which are at the same time similar and yet different. This is precisely what is expressed in Saussure's distinction between *langue* and *parole*, one being the structural side of language, the other the statistical aspect of it, *langue* belonging to a reversible time, *parole* being non-reversible. If those two levels already exist in language, then a third one can conceivably be isolated. (Lévi-Strauss, 1963, p. 209)

Lévi-Strauss suggests that there are "gross constituent units" in any myth, which he terms "mythemes". He further proposes that mythemes are not single isolated aspects of a myth but "bundles of relations" (in my analogy, the logs that the beavers use to build their dam) (Lévi-Strauss, 1963, p. 211). These relations are connected either "synchronically—at the same time" or "diachronically" at different times, rather as in music there is often harmony and melody at the same time and furthermore, there may be an overall pattern as in a symphony. Thus, Lévi-Strauss says, we can treat the Oedipus myth like an orchestra score. Here is the Oedipus myth in its less well-known extended form laid out according Lévi-Strauss's theory:

Cadmos seeks
his sister Europa,
ravished by Zeus

Cadmos kills
the dragon

The Spartoi kill
one another

Labdacos
(Laios' father)
= *lame* (?)

Oedipus kills his
father, Laios

Laios (Oedipus'
father) = *left-
sided* (?)

Oedipus kills
the Sphinx

Oedipus =
swollen-foot (?)

Oedipus marries
his mother,
Jocasta

Eteocles kills
his brother,
Polynices

Antigone buries
her brother,
Polynices, despite
prohibition

(Lévi-Strauss, 1963, p. 214)

As Lévi-Strauss points out, this layout gives us the opportunity to read the myth in the normal manner by starting at the top left hand corner and then going left to right and down the page. If we examine the myth by reading down each of the columns, then a new series of relationships comes to light.

Lévi-Strauss claims that each column has a common feature. Thus the column on the left is concerned with *the overrating of blood relations*, the next with *the underrating of blood relations*, the third refers to *monsters and their destruction* and the fourth refers to *difficulties in walking straight and standing upright*. The contradictory nature of columns one and two is obvious. However, the contradictory relationship of columns three and four is less clear. Starting with column three, both the dragon and the sphinx are creatures which have to be killed in order that man can be born, thus they refer to the autochthonous origins of man—the original inhabitants are deemed to be men. In column four, therefore, we find the negation of column three. If the dragon and sphinx have been killed by man, then man cannot be the original inhabitants of the earth, some alien being was there before them. A common theme in mythology is the following; when men are born from the Earth—they emerge from the depths (from the mother's womb)—either they cannot walk at all (the condition of the human newborn) or they walk clumsily (the condition of the pre-Oedipal toddler). This is an interesting mythical version of the problem Freud sets himself in *Inhibitions Symptoms and Anxiety*—which comes first, the chicken or the egg, repression or anxiety? Here is Lévi-Strauss's analysis of the problem approached from the direction of anthropology:

> The myth has to do with the inability, for a culture which holds the belief that mankind is autochthonous . . . to find a satisfactory transition between this theory and the knowledge that human beings are actually born from the union of man and woman. Although the problem obviously cannot be solved the Oedipus myth provides a kind of logical tool which relates the original problem—born from one or born from two?—to the derivative problem: born from different or born from same? By a correlation of this type, the overrating of blood relations is to the underrating of blood relations as the attempt to escape autochthony is the impossibility to succeed in it. Although experience contradicts

theory, social life validates cosmology by its similarity of structure. Hence cosmology is true. (Lévi-Strauss, 1953, p. 216)

Lévi-Strauss goes on to elaborate these ideas in order to derive a formula for myth. The many formulae Lévi-Strauss has devised for the elaboration of myth have been attacked on several grounds, perhaps most particularly the lack of correlation between individual cultural practice and the generalisations he attempts to make. However, this I think is to miss a fundamental point. Lévi-Strauss is arguing that myths as a whole serve key functions in the fantasies and anxieties of groups of people. The variations between groups may be enormous and the mytheme (Lévi-Strauss's term for the constituent elements of myths) may be too generalised a tool to account for such variations. Put simply: we find myths in all cultures (even if they do not always appear with this label) and myths are there for good reasons—principally to keep anxiety under control.

Incidentally, another implication of Lévi-Strauss's theory is that it offers a credible explanation for Forster's illustration of the vagaries of listening to music. If a myth is construed like a symphonic score, then it cannot be read both synchronically and diachronically *at the same time.* For Forster, and I suspect for most music lovers, listening to music involves paying attention either to one aspect of music making at a time and sometimes involves not hearing it at all; yet there is a co-ordinating background function operating whilst we listen that enables us to leave a concert with a coherent impression of the evening. Freud's account of the efforts of the ego to present us with a unified impression of its inevitably fragmented parts comes to mind again.

The structure of a myth, therefore, is neither random nor accidental. As both Freud and Lacan indicate, the route through the Oedipus complex is a necessity that produces fantasy formations in the individual so that she/he can negotiate the daily experience of life in a way that enables sense and meaning to be imported into their daily thinking, activity, and indeed, dreaming. Consequently, Lévi-Strauss argues that the structuring effects of the Oedipus complex are reflected in the structure of the Oedipus myth itself.

The key elements of Lévi-Strauss's arguments have all kinds of implications for a study of the structure of the unconscious. Freud more than once makes the assertion that there is no negation in the unconscious. However, as we saw in chapter one, he puts forward a series of arguments that qualify this statement. As the Lévi-Strauss quotation above indicates, we are back in the territory of the apparent contradictions spelled out in Freud's paper, in other words, the absence of a means of representing negation and contradiction in the unconscious whilst in some senses contradiction is clearly and alive (if not well) and kicking in the preconscious and the conscious. Lévi-Strauss's theory offers us the opportunity to see negation at work not simply at the level of an individual's story but also as part of the account that groups give of themselves in order to make the world more explicable and more livable. Hollywood films abhor unhappy endings for precisely this reason.

If we are to make the link between Freud and Lévi-Strauss even more apparent, then at this point, we need to return to Freud's *The Interpretation of Dreams*. Freud's theory of negation has an operational function in consciousness, and the question arises as to its relation to the unconscious as revealed or concealed in the dream. In 1900 Freud's view seems straightforward, "the way in which dreams treat the category of contraries and contradictories is highly remarkable. It is simply disregarded" (Freud, 1900a, p. 318). Freud continues in a footnote on the same page:

> I was astonished to learn from a pamphlet by K. Abel, *The Antithetical Meaning of Primal Words* (1884) . . . that the most ancient languages behave exactly like dreams in this respect. In the first instance they have only a single word to describe the two contraries at the extreme ends of a series of qualities or activities (e.g. "strong-weak", "old-young", "far-near", "bind-sever"); they only form distinct terms for the two contraries by a secondary process of making small modifications in the common word . . . (Freud, 1900a, pp. 318–19)

If we assume that a myth has the relation to a group that a dream has to an individual, then, oscillating between Lévi-Strauss and Freud, a myth can be construed as offering a series of "small modifications". The contradictions are concealed in the form of a story, rather as Freudian "considerations of representability " or "dramatisation" are an essential part of the dream work that translates the latent unacceptable aspect of a dream into something that looks harmless (such as "the tall story" alluded to above) to the slightly less watchful sleeping ego. We therefore arrive at the conclusion that, like dreams, myths are a method of dealing with difficult and problematic aspects of human experience denied in the unconscious.

However, in his paper "Negation", published in 1925, Freud's early view that the unconscious disregards contraries and contradictories has changed somewhat. He suggests that, "Negation is a way of taking cognizance of what is repressed; indeed it is already a lifting of the repression, though not, of course an acceptance of what is repressed" (Freud, 1925h, pp. 235–6). Thus, negation and denial are not necessarily the same thing, a point that Freud also makes in this brief but important paper. A denial, therefore, in a sense is a denial of difference. (This is also, incidentally, the reason for consulting the French version of the Lévi-Strauss text.)

* * *

Thus far, I have considered the role of fantasy in the construction of plot or myth making in the Freudian sense of employing the use of negation to establish difference and I have rejected Susan Isaacs and her colleagues since a monolithic approach to fantasy allows for no plot development. Lévi-Strauss's theory gives a much more credible account of how human beings in groups develop stories and myths.

Finally I wish to return to a psychoanalytic concept beloved of Freud and Lacan, the notion of the drive. Paul Verhaeghe's recounts the following scenario in a chapter appropriately entitled "Dreams between drive and desire":

> A patient consults his analyst because of a recurrent dream, "Doctor, doctor, every night last week I dreamt that I entered the bedroom of my new neighbour and fucked her senseless. I don't understand this, what does it mean?"
>
> The analyst answers, "It means that you want to ride a white horse through your neighbour's front garden armed with a long black spear." (Verhaeghe, 2001, p. 134 *my editing*)

Verhaeghe then remarks upon the fact that at one level there is much less repression around than in 1900. He reminds us of Freud's interesting statement that I have paraphrased below:

There is often a passage in even the most thoroughly interpreted dream which has to be left obscure . . . there is a tangle of dream-thoughts which cannot be unravelled . . . this is the dream's navel, the spot where it reaches down into the unknown . . . it is at some point where this meshwork is particularly close that the dream-wish grows up, like a mushroom out of its mycelium. (Freud, 1900a, p. 525)

He then proposes a Lacanian reading of Freud:

Firstly: every dream contains a double level, where on the one hand we have the level of desire, and on the other hand the level of jouissance. Secondly: these two levels correspond to two different layers in the unconscious, i.e. the repressed unconscious and the original or system Ucs. Thirdly: this double level obliges us to reconsider the therapeutic goals of analysis. (Verhaeghe, 2001, p. 135)

The heart of the argument concerns the nature of the navel or kernel of the dream. Is it or is it not linguistic? Early Lacan would indicate an affirmative answer. However, the Conference at Bonneval marked a turning point. Laplanche and Leclaire argued for a linguistic kernel to the system unconscious, whereas Lacan then started to develop a theory based on that part of the unconscious that Freud had conceptualised as never having been repressed. The objet *a*—that which eludes signification—becomes an increasing preoccupation. Verhaeghe then shows how drive theory has to be linked to dream theory—the navel of the dream—the abyss or "gap" is also the origin of the drive and as such is not symbolisable.

Returning to the world of fantasy, then the question now arises: how does the drive operate on fantasy? Roberto Harari's book, *Lacan's Seminar on "Anxiety": An Introduction* extends Lévi-Strauss's concept of mythemes to phantemes. He expands upon the notions of fantasy in the Laplanche and Leclaire paper which links fantasy to the key Freudian elements seduction, castration and the primary scene and suggests the following correspondences:

Phanteme	*a*
return to the womb	breast
seduction	faeces

castration	phallus
primal scene	gaze
family novel	voice

(Harari, 2001, p. 232)

In this formulation, therefore, we have bundles (beavers' log-piles) of phantasmatic relations, each of which refer to a different aspect of the drive. Harari's commentary on the Anxiety seminar is engrossing and fascinating but it lacks a clinical dimension. Verhaeghe hints at an answer. He suggests that it lies in Lacan's seminar, *The Sinthome*. Thus, the task of a contemporary analysis becomes one where the analysand creates his own story, his own signifier that "knots the registers of the Real, the Symbolic and the Imaginary together into a particular sexual rapport". (Verhaeghe 2001, p. 144) The sinthome is an archaic version of the French "symptôme", and the task of analysis is to identify with the sinthome, as Luke Thurston puts it, "a kernel of enjoyment immune to the efficacy of the symbolic". (Evans, 1996, p. 189)

However, we are a step removed from analysis itself. What are the clinical mechanisms that describe the manner in which the analysand can identify with his/her sinthome? It is possible to descend into a series of platitudes about interpretation, free association and so on. Alternatively, the Kleinian route would be simply to declare that all is phantasy and all that can be done is to weaken the power of the infantile phantasies by interpreting their true nature to the patient. However, this is unfair to a complex and fruitful body of ideas. Picking up the concept of mythemes from Lévi-Strauss and developing this notion, fantasies can be considered as complex bundles of relations that operate, often in conflict, in the Symbolic, the Imaginary and the Real.

From here we will turn from an account of the plot to stories themselves. In the next chapter we will look at the different themes to be found in the genres of the gothic, sci-fi and in the literature on utopias. The construction of the plot is only part of the story.

CHAPTER FIVE

Gothic tales and other stories

"Have you," she said, "seen the portraits in the house of my fathers? Have you looked at my mother or at Felipe? Have your eyes never rested on that picture that hangs by your bed? She who sat for it died ages ago; and she did evil in her life. But, look again: there is my hand to the least line, there are my eyes and my hair. What is mine, then, and what am I? If not a curve in this poor body of mine (which you love, and for the sake of which you dotingly dream that you love me), not a gesture that I can frame, not a tone of my voice, not any look from my eyes, no, not even now when I speak to him I love, but has belonged to others? Others, ages dead, have wooed other men with my eyes; other men have heard the pleading of the same voice that now sounds in your ears. The hands of the dead are in my bosom; they move me, they pluck me, they guide me; I am a puppet at their command; and I but reinform features and attributes that have long been laid aside from evil in the quiet of the grave. Is it me you love, friend? Or the race that made me? The girl who does not know and cannot answer for the least portion of herself? Or the stream of which she is a transitory eddy, the tree of which she is the passing fruit? The race exists; it is old, it is very young, it carries its eternal destiny in its bosom; upon it, like waves upon the sea, individual succeeds to individual, mocked with a semblance of self-control, but they are nothing. We speak of the soul, but the soul is in the race." (Stevenson, 1885, pp. 210–11)

Robert Louis Stevenson's short story, "Olalla", combines all the classic ingredients of the gothic—contradiction, ambiguity, life in death and rampant sexuality. This extract contains all of these elements and, through these means, creates an atmosphere of increasing tension. Is Olalla young and beautiful or supernaturally old? Dead hands in reality cannot move; yet, they move, pluck and guide Olalla. Is she a puppet at the hands of others or is she "re-informing" features long dead by seemingly giving them life? Is Olalla a new phenomenon and part of a new race of beings or an age-old throwback? Gothic horror in splendid writing such as this brings negative dialectics vividly to "undead" life.

From plot to tale

The previous chapter explored what happens when we "lose the plot" in our own internal world. Yet, of course, the domain of fantasy is not simply limited to the stories we create for our own private consumption in our minds. Shared fantasies have a long history, starting with myth and legend, and then progressing with ever increasing variety to the rich cultural mix found anywhere and everywhere that supports human life. In earlier chapters, the fantasies we create in the privacy of our minds were explored demonstrating some of the complex relationships between one fantasy and another and their role in coping with our anxieties.

Having looked at the construction of plots in our minds, can we learn anything from the structure and content of the fantasies that are everywhere available for our collective entertainment, whether they are TV programmes, films, computer games or even old-fashioned books? Are fantasies something more than simple entertainment to fill up our TV and cinema screens or to while away our time on computer games? Does fantasy just occur arbitrarily in our cultural life for equally arbitrary reasons, or is there a kind of unconscious logic at work here, a logic which uses this wealth of cultural artefacts as weapons in an armoury of fantasies directed at mitigating, transmuting or even dispelling our anxieties?

Today, commercialised fantasies are everywhere. Indeed, in much of the modern world, we are living in a period of "fantasy excess" on TV with an endless diet of soaps, police procedurals, personal and house makeovers, and travel and cooking programmes. I have deliberately included in this list some programmes that are often described as "reality TV" because, in truth, they often encourage the viewer to dream of living in a place they will never visit, preparing a dish they will never eat, and fraternising with people the likes of whom they would probably never otherwise get to meet. Yet, in this time of apparent glut, there are also those who complain of a dearth of the "real thing"—fantasy as truly imaginative and nourishing food for the soul. From the "glut" we shall select three kinds of fantasy that can be shown to have a clear relationship to the way individuals fantasise, since, in different ways they generate effective responses to anxieties shared by many of us.

The gothic fantasy is particularly interesting from a psycho-analytic point of view, since it offers a number of insights into our simultaneous preoccupation with and avoidance of death. The death instinct/drive is a key psychoanalytic theme, which produces heated and lively debates about its very existence! The gothic also exem-plifies, as the quotation from "Olalla" demonstrates, the constant alternation between themes of life and death just as in the first chap-ter we explored the oscillation inherent in themes of negation in general. This chapter will argue that the gothic offers an opportunity for us to explore negation in our "public" fantasies as well as our private ones.

The latter half of the chapter will differentiate the structure of gothic fantasies from science fiction and utopias and their *alter egos*, dystopias. Since they all deal with anxiety in one shape or another, there are many similarities between these fantasy genres, but also interesting differences.

The ingredients of gothic fantasy

In the introduction to this book, the opening quotation from Words-worth set the tone for the description of a subtle change in much western culture that has taken place over the last two hundred and fifty years. Before the advent of the novel and one of its early derivatives, the gothic tale, much storytelling in the western world centred on religious themes. *The Canterbury Tales* is united by the religious motif of the pilgrimage even if the contents of many of the tales are clearly secular, not to say bawdy. As the next chapter on religion will show, religious ideas have often changed but they have by no means disappeared. However, the spread of atheism and agnosticism has fuelled the appetite for fantasies that occupy a place formerly taken by religion. The fact that the novel, including the gothic novel, became very fashionable in Europe in the 1790s after the French revolution, and has remained so ever since, can be connected to this appetite.

This early connection to religion is further exemplified by the religious overtones discernable in common gothic themes. Everything is shrouded in mystery, the palette of colour ranges from funereal purple to bloody scarlet and deepest black. In the gothic world, things "that go bump in the night" are accompanied by the dreadful screams of the terrified victims; howls of ghoulish pleasure from the wicked perpetrators of unspeakable crimes are *de rigueur*. This mirrors some of the lurid horrors conjured up by condemnation and punishment of witches, the visions of the damned rotting in hell and the notorious activities of the Inquisition. Just as in religion, the links to death are everywhere; blood, blackness and the uncertain arbitrary experience of life itself are not only brought to the fore— they are enhanced by dramatic artifice and spine tingling music. Music often plays a key part in religious ritual and is now our constant companion in everyday life. It can dramatically change our emotional reactions. *Psycho* would be a rather tame movie without the terrifying screeches of the film track accompanying the gory and somewhat gothic scene in the shower. As every fan instinctively understands, a key to the enjoyment of the gothic fantasy is revelling in the uncertainties of whether creatures such as Dracula and his colleagues among the "undead" are *really* alive or dead: the same ambiguity applies to their victims. Even today, the religious believer can keep doubts about life after death at bay by singing sentiments epitomised by the famous Handel aria, "I know, I know my Redeemer liveth" in a spirit of optimistic hopefulness. The music reinforces both the emotion and the sentiment.

In Chris Baldick's excellent essay on gothic tales, he argues that gothic fantasy has a preventive function. Exercising (or exorcising?) a fantasy prevents us from dwelling too literally on the possibility of the real horrors that may await us in our nightmares although not normally in reality, "Gothic fiction is a way of exercising such anxieties, but also of allaying them by imagining the worst before it can happen, and giving it at least a safely recognizable form" (Baldick,

1992, p. xxii). It is also a kind of denial of the true impact of death on those who are left behind. Such a theme is similarly present in many religions where one can say, hopefully but perhaps rather untruthfully, "O death where is thy sting?"

Returning to the theme of contradiction and negation highlighted in the opening extract from "Olalla", this echoes the theme of chapter one. It is a vivid account of negative dialectics in action. Baldick illuminates this point further; he details the series of oppositions that many gothic tales contain:

> Long after they [the Goths] disappeared into the ethnic melting-pots of the northern Mediterranean, their fearful name was taken and used to prop up one side of that set of cultural oppositions by which the Renaissance and its heirs defined and claimed possession of European civilization: Northern versus Southern, Gothic versus Graeco-Roman, Dark Ages versus the Age of Enlightenment, medieval versus modern, barbarity versus civility, superstition versus Reason. (Baldick, 1992, p. xii)

In each pairing, gothic fantasy represents the darker more sinister aspect of human perception and addresses a fear by means of sub-stitution: the gothic fantasy of death permitting a kind of undead life to continue, stands in for the real dread and horror of death as a dead end with no possibility of continuity. Thus far, we have characterised the gothic via its oppositional qualities reminiscent of negative dialectics combined with its black, tragic, dark and necrophilic aspects. The dramatization inherent in gothic tales also warrants attention. This is evident even in the mode of presentation of the earliest tale identified with the gothic tradition, Hugh Walpole's *The Castle of Otranto* in 1764. In an introduction to the text, E. J. Clery writes:

> The significance of *Otranto* for literary history lies as much in the two Prefaces and their alternative constructions of the text as antiquity or innovation, as it does in the novel itself. Readers of the first edition had been led to believe that it was written by a scheming priest, bent on encouraging superstition "in the darkest ages of Christianity"; now, with the initials "H.W." added to the second edition, it was discovered to be the work of a living

Member of Parliament and prominent figure in fashionable
society. (Clery, 1998, pp. xi–xii)

No doubt, this preface contributed to the sales of this work since it
is already rendering the subject matter mysterious and fascinating
before the reader has even started reading the story! Walpole's novel
is not widely read nowadays, since the kindest of contemporary
readers would be hard put to assert that Walpole had any talents
at all as a novelist. He is remembered as an innovator of a form of
literature, not for being a skilled exponent of the form. Dark and
dramatic secrets are an essential ingredient of gothic novels and they
also make good publicity material. Perhaps Walpole should rather
be remembered as an early publicist!

A few years later, Ann Radcliffe's highly dramatic gothic classic,
The Mysteries of Udolpho was a runaway best seller. In the introduction
to the Oxford's world classics edition, Terry Castle comments:

What accounted for Udolpho's extraordinary appeal? A clue may
lie in the key word of its title: mysteries. Radcliffe, one might
argue, was a purveyor of mysteries—but of a new kind, adapted
for a secular age. Her book itself is a kind of mystery-machine,
of course, full of local puzzles and conundrums. Who has stolen
the miniature of Emily in the book's opening chapters? What is
in her dead father's secret papers? Who walks the ramparts at
night under her window at Udolpho? . . . And so on. For much
of the novel, as the uncertainties pile up, we are indeed Mother
Radcliffe's children: lost in a cloud of unknowing. (Castle, 1998,
In Radcliffe, 1794, p. xxi)

A psychoanalyst might point out that Radcliffe's novel is a beautifully
tailored unconscious response to changing cultural needs. If we do
away with religious belief, we do not do away with death at the same
time. We still need a mechanism which will temper our anxieties on
this score.

Jane Austen wrote *Northanger Abbey* as a parody on the then pre-
vailing fashion for gothic novels and Radcliffe's novel, in particular.
The key characters in *Northanger Abbey* have all read or are in the
process of reading *The Mysteries of Udolpho* and its imitators: some
of them avidly consumed such stories like present-day computer

game aficionados. Austen's naïve heroine, Catherine Morland, half-believes that the lurid descriptions of secrets concealed on parchment in the drawers of locked chests, mysterious goings on in ancient haunted ruins and wicked men eager to do away with defence-less women, are really true—shades of those who think that the characters in TV soaps are "real". Thus, Catherine is tempted to imagine that General Tilney, the father of the hero will turn out to have dramatically disposed of his wife under suspicious circumstances. As the novel progresses, the death of Tilney's wife turns out to be the result of natural causes and, contrary to Catherine's assumptions, the General is actually saddened by his wife's death. The eponymous Northanger Abbey is full of noises caused by wind and rain but there is no evidence of haunting and rather distressingly for Catherine, the house has recently been modernised! Austen's powers of satire are beautifully illustrated in the scene where Catherine manages to open a mysterious chest by candlelight and finds some sheets of paper with curious hieroglyphics—only to find in the light of day that they are old laundry bills.

The novel makes an interesting and sophisticated distinction between real and manufactured *fear*. The mystery element is a secondary motif in Austen's text. Catherine "believes" in a world of gothic high romance created in likes of *The Mysteries of Udolpho*. Her *fears* of what she will find when she visits Northanger Abbey, the Tilney family home, are stimulated as a result. Henry Tilney and his sister Eleanor persuade Catherine to give up her groundless fears through gentle teasing; they also supply her with the mundane facts of their mother's death due to illness. However, the exposure to the fears engendered by the gothic novel do not prepare Catherine or save her from the fears connected to the humiliation and shame that she experiences when confronted by a real crisis—being asked to leave the Tilneys' house in disgrace without explanation:

> Heavily past [sic] the night. Sleep, or repose that deserved the name of sleep, was out of the question. That room, in which her disturbed imagination had tormented her on her first arrival, was again the scene of agitated spirits and unquiet slumbers. Yet how different now the source of her inquietude from what it had been then—how mournfully superior in reality and substance! Her anxiety had foundation in fact, her fears in probability; and with

a mind so occupied in the contemplation of actual and natural
evil, the solitude of her situation, the darkness of her chamber,
the antiquity of the building were felt and considered without
the smallest emotion; and though the wind was high, and often
produced strange and sudden noises throughout the house, she
heard it all as she lay awake, hour after hour, without curiosity
or terror. (Austen, 1817, p. 198)

Catherine may not have curiosity or terror, but as a result, she is
afraid to return home because she does not know what she will find
there. Will her family too, criticise her for some unexplained
misdemeanour? Her fear is only relieved when her family greet her
with warmth and affection.

To return to the parodic elements of the plot, the "villain" of
Northanger Abbey is not General Tilney; he may be a snobbish autocrat
but he is also a bereaved husband. A comically drawn subsidiary
character, John Thorpe is the "villain" in the sense of being cause of
Catherine's romantic troubles. Austen sketches him as a thoroughly
recognizable contemporary-sounding young man of limited imagination and a tedious preoccupation with showing off his driving
skills and boasting about the pecuniary wealth of his acquaintances.
The satirical elements of the novel are grounded in the contrast
between Catherine's gothic flights of fancy and the everyday
ordinariness of her experience.

There is, however, a sense in which *Northanger Abbey* is actually
just as much a creation of fantasy as *The Mysteries of Udolpho*, the
novel it parodies. After all, it is a novel with touches of romantic
fantasying that do not belong to the "real" world of the early 1800s—
it has a "happily ever after" ending. As in all of Austen's major
works, the heroine gets her man, when in real life at that time, the
chances are that Henry Tilney would simply have accepted his
father's edict to marry solely for money and position and never
contacted Catherine again.

We need to look at the distinctions between the fears engendered
by the gothic fictions that are satirized and the "real" fears experienced by Catherine in the novel combined with the phenomenon of
a villain who does not instil fear at all. Austen illustrates for us that
fact that our fears, both in reality and in fantasy, often contain the
seeds of doubt. Indeed, an essential component of fear is precisely

this element of uncertainty—will the heroine die or won't she? The gothic embodies the direct paradox and contradiction of death in life and life in death, but there are other methods of playing upon our fears. Austen contrasts Catherine's real as opposed to her imagined experiences. Thus, there is a further series of oppositions in the relationship between one style of fantasy and another and their separate relation to external reality where those differences are often also shrouded in uncertainty. In satire too, there is a complex relationship between the satirist and what is satirised, between the position of Austen, *The Mysteries of Udolpho* and her heroine Catherine. As Freud demonstrated in *Jokes and their Relation to the Unconscious*, many a true word is spoken in jest and, by the same token, many a true anxiety is dissipated by satire. The juxtaposition of fantasy and reality in the gothic mode may be uneasy and mysterious, but of course it also occurs in other genres.

We now have three themes running through the gothic; internal contradictions in the story, the pre-emptive and thereby preventative approach to dealing with fear through safe exposure to the most frightening of our thoughts and finally the notion of the complex and often deliberately unclear contradiction in the relation of different aspects of gothic fantasying to reality. Thus far, we have not addressed another key feature of the gothic fantasy—the role of sexuality. Chapter two showed how sexuality is instrumental in fixing our desires and thereby formulating our relationship to the world. Fantasies of doubt, not only about fundamentals such as life or death but also about the meaning of sexuality keep fears of something worse at bay. Thorpe could not possibly be a gothic figure; he is not mysterious; he is not sexually repulsive (and thereby attractive in the gothic mode of being); his conversation bores everyone with platitudes and is far too predictable for the purposes of stirring either our imaginations or that of Austen's heroine, Catherine.

Austen takes the opportunity to engage in a polemic with her rivals. She argues that some books are much better than others because they "mimic" reality more closely. She focuses her attack on the ridiculous unreality that pervades novels such as *The Mysteries of Udolpho*. The latter piles one improbable and unlikely event upon another in pursuit of an effect of mystery and fear whereas Austen's *Northanger Abbey* is notable for the subtlety of its exploration of fear and fantasy. It is at least as well constructed as Austen's later more highly regarded novel, *Pride and Prejudice*. For many years, *Northanger Abbey* was one of the least popular of Austen's novels, perhaps because then, as now, both gothic and sci-fi fantasies are often regarded as second rate. Similarly, it is probably no accident that Stevenson is better known for his adventure stories, *Kidnapped* and *Treasure Island* than for writing "Olalla". Perhaps we do not like to remember our debts to the fantasies that work best for us.

Sex and sexuality are only hinted at in *Northanger Abbey*. *Dracula* however is a very different story. If all that Dracula needed was blood—and the blood of any human being would do—then the story would be much closer to the traditional adventure story. Bram Stoker's novel is full of dashing young men and swooning female victims. The drawing of blood by Dracula, in the transparently sexual and darkened surroundings of the bedroom at night produces a frisson. Sex and death make good bedfellows in our fantasy world, and sometimes in the "real" world, because, as Freud and others have pointed out, we spend our lives in a constant oscillation between the urge to life inherent in sex and the inexorable progress towards dying inherent in being mortal. The oscillation sets up an uneasy disjuncture. Dracula solves this problem by achieving what is in reality impossible—a sexual life in the midst of death, to be feared and savoured at one and the same time.

Sex and sexuality is the subject of fascinating distinctions in *Dracula*. Bizarrely, no few than three men propose to one of the heroines, Lucy Westenra, and none of them ever have sex with her. During the events of the novel, the principal female characters, Lucy and Mina never have genital sex with a man. Dracula is a character whose sexual desires are satisfied by the oral—he bites his victims. Symbolisation of genital sexuality occurs only in events such as the slaying of Dracula, "But, on the instant, came the sweep and flash of Jonathan's great knife. I shrieked as I saw it shear through the throat; whilst at the same moment Mr. Morris's bowie knife plunged into the heart" (Stoker, 1897, p. 367).

The relationship of the gothic to science fiction

We shall now shift our attention to other forms of fantasy. What differentiates one kind of fictional fantasy from another? Do different forms of fantasy serve different unconscious purposes? Sci-fi, like the gothic, appears in all kinds of cultural guises. It is always set either in another time, or in another world where the constraints of time have been manipulated or shifted in some way. The effect is to defer the moment of death. Thus, *Star Trek* transports us to a year comfortably far in the future: the year is deliberately computed by methods that do not coincide with our calendar in order to increase the illusion of otherworldliness. 46379.1 is a star date and "Trekkie" websites are dedicated to making dates like this "fit" with each other in terms of the various events in the history of the *Star Trek* programmes. The monsters, aliens, the Borg may be intended to terrify, but since they do not attack *now*, we can comfortably sit back, secure in the knowledge that what we see on our screens is not happening in the present. The precise date does not matter except to more obsessional fans of the programmes.

On the other hand, in gothic fantasy, the past, embodied in ruins, crenellated castles and the like, continually threatens to reappear, lurching unwanted and unwelcomed (but nevertheless of course awaited with eager anticipation) into the present. In science fiction and fantasy, time is conveniently shifted forwards from the here and now or sideways to a parallel world; its effects are denied in the process and the past is a deliberately vague and undefined country. In the gothic world, the effects of the past on the present are not only ubiquitous but also exaggerated.

The principal characters in any version of *Star Trek* hardly ever die, despite the fact that their missions encounter danger at the very least on a regular weekly basis. Death is always avoided, deferred to another day, another time. By contrast, the gothic does not avoid death, its overriding theme is death itself, meted out to good and evil characters alike. Gothic fantasies are laden with sexual imagery; as we have seen, *Dracula* always sinks his fangs into young and beautiful women, a series of sexual meetings before their death in life or life in death. In *Civilization and its Discontents*, Freud concluded that:

> ... [T]he meaning of evolution of civilization is no longer obscure to us. It must present the struggle between Eros and Death, between the instinct of life and the instinct of destruction, as it works itself out in the human species. This struggle is what all life essentially consists of, and the evolution of civilization

may therefore be simply described as the struggle for life of the human species. And it is this battle of the giants that our nurse-maids try to appease with their lullaby about Heaven. (Freud, 1930a, p. 122)

Death is the price we pay for our consciousness and our sexuality. In the gothic and in sci-fi our resultant anxieties are dealt with by different means. A gothic solution serves to enhance our awareness of the struggle between Eros and Death and render it harmless as it were, by inoculation. A sci-fi solution is to endlessly defer the existence of death. Thus, in *Dracula* and in other classic gothic tales such as the quotation from "Olalla" at the start of this chapter, anxiety is allayed by, returning to Baldick's words, "imagining the worst before it can happen" (Baldick, 1992, p. xxii). In *Star Trek* anxieties are allayed by a change in the time-frame and the "humanity" frame; our fears are not courted but displaced. Since death is not an option, the heroes of *Star Trek* never panic: in this regard; in one sense they are as "inhuman" as their monstrous enemies. Apparently they live forever in a time-warp limbo.

Yet paradox and contradiction are just as inherent to science fiction as they are to the gothic. The subject matter of the contradictions changes and thereby the nature of the fears that are addressed. A curious feature is the human behaviour that motivates even the most inhuman robot. One of *Star Trek's* most famous enemies, The Borg, still possess human as well as robotic qualities since they have the very human characteristic of desire, even if that desire is to rid the universe of human beings! Human beings constantly have deal with the fact that not only do they wish to live forever; they also want to deprive others of this illusory opportunity by killing them. When the Daleks in *Dr Who* chant, "Exterminate! Exterminate!" our interest in slaughter has been cleverly and safely transferred to a robot. Another point of view would be that Daleks are "anti-humans" and represent the following equation: no mortality = no morality = no thinking = not being human. Whether human behaviour is transferred or abstracted through equation, either way, these alien life forms remain surprisingly human in conception. Even the strangest being bears some resemblance in ways of (often murderous) thinking, to humans. Sci-fi demonstrates that as human beings, we can only think within the framework of what it means to be human in the first place. Like the gothic, it makes a valiant attempt to mitigate a key aspect of the anxiety-provoking experience of being human. Yet, as Freud's concept of the return of the repressed demonstrates, the darker impulses of humanity haunt both sci-fi and the gothic.

A similar argument applies to sex in both sci-fi and gothic fantasy. If the gothic has an excess of sexual frisson, there is something very sexless about science fiction. None of the characters of *Star Trek* is obviously sexually attractive and affairs of the heart play a very minor part in the plots. In real life, sex not only brings the varied pleasures of physical sexual acts to human beings, it plays an essential part in the bringing into being of human emotions. The emotional charge, if any, in *Star Trek* is not centred primarily on the human figures in the story. It is usually to be found in the interaction between the humans and the other life forms. In both genres, sexuality is often formulaic. *Buffy the Vampire Slayer* was a cult TV gothic series that filled a different niche from *Star Trek*. In Buffy herself, we have a sexually attractive character, drawn to a clearly attractive half-vampire half vampire-slayer figure called Angel (surely a deliberate choice of name). Much of the plotting resembles straightforward action movies and the preoccupation with the past is not strongly featured, yet death in life and life in death remain consistent themes of the series.

However, a more subtle and "lifelike" approach to issues of sexuality can sometimes be found at least in gothic fantasy. Iain Banks writes novels with gothic and/or supernatural themes and under the name Iain M. Banks, straight science fiction. His disturbing account of deliberately altered sexual identity in *The Wasp Factory* makes compelling reading. The pages of this novel clarify better than many a psychoanalytic text some of the complex relationships between gender, sex and death:

> In the bathroom, after a piss, I went through my daily washing ritual. First I had my shower. The shower is the only time in any twenty-four-hour period I take my underpants right off. I put the old pair in the dirty-linen bag in the airing cupboard. I showered carefully, starting at my hair and ending between my toes and under my toenails. Sometimes, when I have to make precious substances such as toenail cheese or belly-button fluff, I have to

go without a shower or bath for days and days; I hate doing this because I soon feel dirty and itchy, and the only bright thing about such abstinence is how good it feels to have a shower at the end of it. (I. Banks, 1984, p. 44)

And

The murders were my own conception; my sex. The Factory was my attempt to construct life, to replace the involvement which otherwise I did not want.

Well, it is always easier to succeed at death. (I. Banks, 1984, p. 183)

Compare this with the following brief extract from his science fiction novel, *Consider Phlebas*:

In the darkness of the cabin, on a small bed full of strange scents and new textures, they performed the same old act, theirs—they both knew—an almost inevitably barren cross-matching of species and cultures thousands of light-years apart. Then they slept. (I. M. Banks, 1987, p. 82)

In *The Wasp Factory*, the account of the narrator's relationship to his body is detailed, individual and intimate. The second quotation from the book draws our attention with admirable economy to the intertwining of sex, murder and death. In Banks and perhaps in other writers too, the science fiction genre encourages considerations of issues on the grand scale, such as the place of culture and sex in the lives of whole galaxies. His stories in the gothic mode concentrate on the place of the individual and the family in the wider culture. The change of genre produces a different reaction to the sexual. It is much more central to the concerns of the individual exemplified in the gothic than to the culture at large exemplified in sci-fi. In his science fiction writing, Banks writes sex scenes between semi-human beings that are much less compelling; they are impersonal and rather automatic. The reference to the biological fact that species which are not closely related cannot produce children seems dutiful rather than interesting.

Similarities between gothic and sci-fi

Sci-fi and the gothic have striking similarities as well as differences. Violence is a common feature. One of the reasons for watching any gothic inspired film is the thrill of watching Dracula stalk his victims and listening to the blood-curdling shrieks that accompany his success. Similarly, *Star Trek* would not have a plot line if the aliens simply greeted Captain Jean-Luc Picard by saying (in faultless English), "Welcome to our planet, make yourselves at home for as long as you like and we'll help you write a report for the folks back at home".

Fictional fantasy of all kinds has the great advantage of instant gratification. In real life, little that is connected with pleasurable experiences can change as quickly as we would like, but in the life of our wishes and fantasies we can play havoc with the dictates of time and change our selection of fantasy on a whim to suit our personal tastes. It is at least suggestive that we form our cultural preferences in response to unconscious anxiety just as much as with conscious enjoyment. If this is not the case, then it becomes very hard to explain why the same plot lines, themes and types of fantasy constantly recur.

Our fantasy preferences indicate the lure of desire, the lure of opening up the wish for change—if only I could wake up and find that various unpalatable facts pertaining to my life had been changed for me overnight without any effort on my part. Captain Jean-Luc Picard of the *Starship Enterprise* perfectly enacts this fantasy when he says to the computer, "make it so". So many people wish that they could simply "make it so", or make their lives otherwise. Psychoanalytic patients often wish they could be over and done with analysis in a couple of hours. However, the wish to play around with timing in our fantasies is a poisoned chalice. Despite our wish to stand still, to go back in time or to stop the world because we want to get off, none of these options is available to us in reality. Time comes back to haunt us in the form of death.

Both gothic and sci-fi are action packed with deadly and death-like creatures whether they are vampires or exterminating robots. The gothic is an example of death in life or should it be life in death? Yet, the characters in Gothic fantasy often have many characteristics of human beings even if they are "technically" dead. The principal characters in *Buffy the Vampire Slayer* hardly ever "die"—even though they may be technically "dead", they are reassuringly back on our TV screens again the following week. We can relax, secure in the knowledge that even if we identify with them, *we* are not *really* dead. In *Dr Who*, the Daleks are not alive, yet they have all-too-human impulses to kill everything in their path. Again, reassuringly, the key human characters always survive to fight another day and the Daleks always return to resume battle. Everything changes in both gothic and sci-fi fantasy worlds and yet nothing changes. This contrasts with real world where, in the long run, everything is changed by death.

We unconsciously choose our fantasies to represent whatever aspect of sex or death we are either drawn to or repelled by and whether we want to go forwards, backwards or sideways in time. It does not matter whether attraction or repulsion is predominant since these qualities themselves are usually in a dialectical relationship to each other in our minds. Such distinctions may determine whether we prefer sci-fi to gothic fantasy or vice versa, whether we like them equally or whether we avoid fantasies like these as much as possible. Utopias and dystopias are often cast in sci-fi and/or gothic forms; yet they are worth considering separately since they illustrate a particular aspect of fantasy in terms of fantasy's relationship to external reality.

Utopias and dystopias

If the gothic harks back in time and sci-fi is predicated on a time that is not now, it is also possible to take a sideways move offered by utopias and dystopias. Utopias and dystopias can have both gothic and sci-fi characteristics or neither. They can be set in the past, the present or the future and may or may not be imbued with sexual references. Their essential feature lies in imagining that the world in some important sense is *other* than that inhabited by the writer of the fantasy in question. Thomas More's *Utopia* gives a title to the genre and the theme of otherness is indicated by the meaning of "Utopia" in Greek—"no place". Although utopias are intended to be descriptions of an ideal form of human life, characteristically they have a one-dimensional quality and do not give the impression of real lives lived by real people.

More's *Utopia* has a subtext. It was written with a political aim in mind—to criticize the monarchical form of government. Perhaps he hoped that a novel written in Latin would conceal his dissent, but this seems far too simplistic, since the monarch in question, Henry VIII, could read and write Latin fluently. The fact that More was beheaded for refusing to comply with the labyrinthine legal and religious twists required of him by his king so that the latter could wriggle out of one marriage and embark upon the next, is not surprising. What *is* surprising is that More managed to keep his head for so long! The whole book is a devastating critique of what happens when someone, in this case a king, is unable to separate business from pleasure, to separate fact from fantasy, and by virtue of his position to insist upon turning fantasies into facts with devastating consequences as the following two hundred years of British history, including the Civil War, show. More wished that the real world did not contain such problematic issues. The utopian aspects of the book, in terms of the relationships posed between individuals and the state and between men and women, are in some ways incidental to the purpose of the book. In other respects, they represent More's hopes for a better life outside the constraints of monarchy.

A utopia is a species of fantasy, but as Paul Turner points out in the introduction to his 1965 translation of More's *Utopia*, "This emphasis on fantasy is paradoxically combined, as in modern science fiction, with an emphasis on realism" (Turner, In More, 1516, p. 9). Nowadays classic literary utopias and dystopias have fallen out of fashion but the ideas they represent are still very much alive as Žižek points out, ". . . [U]topia has nothing to do with idle dreaming about ideal society in total abstraction from real life: 'utopia' is a matter of innermost urgency, something we are pushed into as a matter of survival, when it is no longer possible to go on within the parameters of the 'possible'" (Žižek, 2004, pp. 123–4). Utopian ideas offer us a dream of society that addresses that aspect of existence that is most unbearable. However, the dream never attains the same status in our thinking as the reality. In 1989, for a short while after the Berlin wall was pulled down, people were ecstatic—utopia had arrived. However, the grinding reality of uniting two different states with widely differing cultural values into one country has sadly of course proved to be anything but utopian. Yet as Žižek might say, this later reality is no longer a matter of survival, more a pragmatic pedestrian conflict between two states, merged idealistically into one, with ideologies lacking the spark of idealism. In other words, the utopian fantasies generated by the fall of the Berlin wall have been snuffed out.

A closely related view of utopias is that they are attempts to imagine an ideal society where perfection, represented by completion of an idea, is attainable. The hero of William Morris's, *News from Nowhere*, the guest, wakes up in a world where people are naturally beautiful; they have arrived "at fashion" to return to the earlier quotation from the Kinks. In Lacanian terms, one could argue that they have arrived at the Real. All the characters in *News from Nowhere* immediately strike us as being highly artificial constructs of Morris's imagination. They are too perfect and far too rational and reasonable.

The background to Morris's work was his lifelong preoccupation with restoring the values of craftsmanship that pertained during the Middle Ages to a Victorian age that was in love with the mass-produced manufactured goods now available as a result of the industrial revolution. The lack of machines in his book is almost comical. For Morris, there was inherent beauty in artefacts produced by human labour and ugliness in the products of mass production. Another theme of *News from Nowhere* is Morris's unhappy marriage to Jane Morris who had a prolonged affair with Dante Gabriel Rossetti; this explains the following extract:

"I know that there used to be such lunatic affairs as divorce courts. But just consider; all the cases that came into them were matters of property quarrels; and I think, dear guest," said he, smiling, "that though you do come from another planet, you can see from the mere outside look of our world that quarrels about private property could not go on amongst us in our days." (Morris, 1891, p. 90)

The novel was originally serialised in a radical magazine entitled *The Commonweal*, but during his lifetime and while writing the novel, Morris became increasingly disillusioned with the way in which life did not imitate art but continued to be nasty, brutish, short and, above all, ugly.

However, as both *Utopia* and *News from Nowhere* unwittingly demonstrate, life is more complicated than art. It could be argued that a defining aspect of fantasy in its utopian aspects is the fact that we would like there to be simple shortcuts to a better reality. The gothic, sci-fi and the utopian ideal all represent simplification either by blurring the clear distinction between life and death as in the gothic or by abstraction from considerations of time and regulation as in sci-fi and utopias. All fantasies are aiming at Lacan's concept of The Real, discussed in chapter three, by trying to eliminate some of the complicated detours insisted upon by external reality. The Real can never be attained. If a utopian ideal moves too close to the Real, instead of identifying with this unreal world, we suspect its perfection and suspiciously unifying characteristics. This reintroduces anxiety. Frightened by the unreality of perfection, either the reader becomes cynical and points to the flaws in the new order or returns like a homing pigeon to that consoling rubric, "It's only a story". Both are strategies of denial of the disturbing nature of otherness. The essence of the Real is, in fact, its sense of disturbing unreality.

Moving from the utopia to the dystopia, their similarities are really more striking than their differences. Neither has room for real people. Utopias start with characters conceived in the style of sci-fi heroes and heroines, far too rational for the real world—and therefore lacking humanity. The plot in dystopias essentially consists in removing the last shreds of humanity from the human. In *Nineteen Eighty-Four*, Winston Smith is reduced to a miserable, snivelling, craven creature —the attributes that made him human have been stripped away by his experiences in Room 101.

What, then, are the differences? The aspirations of the writer in terms of the effect they are hoping to create in the mind of the reader seem to be at play here. Whilst the creator of the dystopia is often consciously exploiting and exposing the inhumanity of the society they actually inhabit, the author of the utopia often seems unaware of the fact that they have excised (exorcised?) key aspects of the human being from the societies they create. Yet, paradoxically, the fallibility of humanity makes its presence felt, taking the author unawares. Morris did not set out to write a novel about his personal preoccupations. He thought he was writing a political tract but, as the extract from *News from Nowhere* above shows, the Freudian repressed returns in the form of Morris's very personal comments about the status and meaning of marriage.

Just a childish dream

Much writing in both the sci-fi and gothic genres is ostensibly aimed at children but in fact read or watched by thousands of adults. In western cultures, people often regard children's thoughts and opinions as "childish"—naive, ill-informed or even stupid and therefore not worthy of serious comment. At the same time, however, the word "childlike" describes a presumed "fantasised(?)" state of innocence that adults often think of rather wistfully. As in so many other instances in this book, a dialectical opposition can be detected in the thinking of many cultures about the place of children in a world dominated by adults. Thus, in Britain, the rating system for films attempts to protect children from seeing sex and violence on the cinema screen—yet attitudes are just as proscribed in theory but in practice much more relaxed when it comes to allowing them to consume alcohol. In the USA, the opposite applies; it seems that frequent episodes of violence on both TV and the big screen is much less of a concern than enforcing their prohibition on under-21 drinking.

The earlier chapter on anxiety featured three different accounts of a phenomenon that Freud termed *Nachträglichkeit* given in the work of Freud himself, Lacan and Laplanche. Despite their differences, these accounts agree that early experiences can play a key role in children's lives. To varying degrees, they perceive these experiences as inherently both traumatic and sexual. In this context, the preventative/pre-emptive aspects of the gothic and sci-fi aspects of children's fantasies can be read as an attempt to deal with what would otherwise be unbearable with regard to death and sexuality.

Contradiction, or the introduction of difference, is not the only means through which children learn. Mimicry of adult behaviour via fantasy is also a striking feature of children's play. The mimicking of reality includes the mimicking of anxiety. Gothic and sci-fi stories deal with our irrational fears and imaginings by dramatising and imitating them. Robots behave like human beings and vampires confuse sex and death. Thus, children pretend to be mummies and daddies, gun-toting robots, characters in the latest TV programme and indeed, whatever else takes their fancy.

In an earlier "pre-gothic" age, Bacon noticed what might now be termed the "gothic" effects prevalent in children's stories, "Men fear death as children fear to go in the dark, and as that natural fear in children is increased with tales, so is the other" (Bacon, 1625, p. 39). One of the most striking characteristics of a gothic tale is its capacity to point to the dark, eerie, frightening aspects of our common fears, highlight them and leave us with a curious frisson of terror, suspense and mystery. At the same time, children and adults enjoy the suspense and the expectation of the worst of our imaginings.

For Bacon at least, these tales do not represent idle thoughts—they do not exist by accident rather than design. He goes on to link the child's fear of the dark with the adult's fear of death—one kind of fear presages another. If the one is afraid of the dark and the other afraid of what the dark represents or conceals—death—this gives us a link between *why* children and adults alike revel in stories of ghosts, the living dead, blood-sucking vampires and so forth. The fears of children resemble the fears of adults but, as psychoanalysts such as Laplanche and Ferenczi have noticed, the *quality* of the fear changes when the *quality* of a personal capacity for sexual experience changes with puberty. It is not surprising then, that both children and adults enjoy gothic and sci-fi fantasies, but for slightly differing reasons. In many films and TV programmes adults laugh at sexual in-jokes that pass children by.

Overall, the fears of both children and adults have not changed much since Bacon's time. Today attempts are sometimes made to make children's literature less frightening and more politically correct. In *Beauty and the Beast,* the treatment of Beauty by the Beast has been construed by some as disguised sexual abuse; but for others it is a tale about the fact that beauty is in the eye of the beholder—what seems ugly at first sight can be beautiful upon closer inspection. *Beauty and the Beast* pales into insignificance compared with the bloodthirsty amoral activities described in many of the stories collected by the Brothers Grimm. Do children's childish/childlike fears need more reassurance? Should we clean up their access to literature just as the Victorians tried to improve upon Shakespeare, for example, by giving *Romeo and Juliet* a happy ending? Should children's fears be cursorily dismissed or on the contrary should they be encouraged? Perhaps this question does not matter since such attempts are doomed to failure. Children invent fantasies to cope with the demands made by a combination of their internal anxieties and their internal fantasy world. The male child who is forbidden to have a toy gun may soon invent "my cricket bat gun" and "my tennis racket gun".

Interestingly these popular debates are in themselves contrary and contradictory—like the gothic itself. "Gothic-style" fears are attacked for using two lines of reasoning. In the first, the concept of reading about notions like life-in-death, death-in-life, vampirism, abduction, imprisonment in dark ruined fortresses and the like is deemed to be childish—adults do not need to read these stories—they are not for "grown-ups". In the second, they are deemed so frightening that they should be expurgated in order that, in effect, children can reside in a fantasy world where their emotions are protected by layers of meaningless fluffy cotton wool. If both of these arguments are carried through to their logical conclusion, it would mean that adults are too adult and children too childish to read or watch gothic fantasy!

Consequently, children's programmes on TV are often a strange mixture of gratuitous violence and sanitised emotions. This is evident from a cartoon within a cartoon. "Itchy and Scratchy" in *The Simpsons* satirises both the classic *Tom and Jerry* and *Mickey Mouse* cartoons, taking the violence to new levels, leaving Bart and Lisa, the older Simpson children, hysterical with laughter. At the other end of the scale, the BBC's programmes for pre-school children such as the *Teletubbies* are vacuous in the extreme. Fortunately, such separation is not always inevitable. Philip Pullman's *His Dark Materials* makes no concessions to the age or indeed the intelligence of his readers. The trilogy is notable for its sophisticated discussion of the problematics of religion and the lovely selection of brief quotations from the likes of Milton, Blake and Rainer Maria Rilke at the beginning of each chapter of the last book in the trilogy, *The Amber Spyglass*. One of the puffs advertising the last novel in the series is by John Pridmore of the Church Times. He says, "Philip Pullman's accomplishment in this great work is to have totally reconceptualised the nature and purpose of fantasy." This seems perhaps too sweeping a claim, but the sexual aspect of these stories constitutes a very sensitive charting of the passage of the experience of love from the perceptions of a child to the more nuanced, stronger and multi-layered sexual perceptions of the adult world. The only surprise is that these novels were originally written primarily for children.

The dichotomy noted at the beginning of this chapter in studying the work of writers such as Robert Louis Stevenson still continues. J. R. R. Tolkien wrote *The Lord of the Rings* as an extended story to read at bedtime to his children, yet his classic is still read and studied by adults. Some take the cult reading of the book to extremes such as learning and conversing in Elvish. Tolkien himself was a professor of Anglo-Saxon and Norse languages and the avoidance of vocabulary with origins in the Romance languages is a feature of the text. The gradually darkening and predominantly sombre tones of much of the story invite the speculation that its composition during the period of the Second World War left a subtle and indelible effect. These two aspects of Tolkien's work might encourage us to treat the book as one just as much intended for adults as for children. It invites the thought: are books for children the better for treating children as adults? Tolkien has no truck with "happily ever after". It is notable that *The Lord of the Rings* ends with the conquest of the forces of darkness but many of the heroic figures of the book have been slain and at the end, Frodo and Gandalf set sail for another kind of world.

Conclusion

In the introduction to this book, I listed some of the denigratory statements about fantasy that people often make such as, "It's just a dream" or "It's only a fantasy." Denigration has a relationship to efficacy in warding off anxiety. Negative dialectics is at work here too. The more effective a fantasy in warding off our anxieties, the more we can afford denigration and denial since we are enabled to feel more secure in our fundamentally insecure world. Similarly, the more complex a fantastic world, the greater the variety of fantasies that are offered to chime with our own particularised needs to fend off anxiety. As indicated in the chapter on religion, our personal preferences when it comes to the choice of TV programmes we watch, the books we read, the films we go to or the computer games we play reflect and complement the unconscious demands of our underlying psychic structure.

Complexity and variety are not everything. It is extremely unfashionable to view length as being in any way an indicator of quality. However, the more complicated and lengthy a fantasy, then the greater the range and duration of its effectiveness may be. At least in part, *The Lord of the Rings* and *The Mysteries of Udolpho* owe their hypnotic capacity to keep us reading not simply to the quality of the storytelling. The reader is distracted from his or her mundane preoccupations with daily life for a considerable length of time. Similarly, *Star Trek* and *Buffy the Vampire Slayer* appear as prolonged series reliably present on our TV screens week after week. Endless deferral of an ending is a good means of keeping the end/death from arriving. This tactic is built into the *Tales of the Arabian Nights* where Scheherazade keeps her head in both senses of the word by telling another tale so beguiling and intriguing that the prince must spare her life for another night so that he can hear what happens next. *Waiting for Godot* . . . As Freud remarked in the context of trauma, that which we do not remember, we are compelled to repeat: we do not "remember" the anxieties defended against by the gothic and sci-fi, but we need constant repetition of the fantasies they enact to keep our anxiety at bay. All fantasies are full of repetitions.

This is a reminder of the process of psychoanalysis with its constant return to the analyst to recapitulate our own private story once more. It can be envisaged as the attempt to put into words some of the fears concealed in our fantasies. Eventually we can tell ourselves a less frightening and punitive tale with a diminished role for our anxieties.

To conclude and lead on to our next theme at the same time, we will return to the relationship of fantasy to religious belief. A text that, perhaps surprisingly characterises this theme is H. G. Wells' classic science fiction novel, *The War of the Worlds*. This is thought by some to be the first genuine science fiction novel. It appeared in 1898, the year before *Dracula*. The narrator in the story provides the following graphic description of his first encounter with an alien from Mars:

Those who have never seen a living Martian can scarcely imagine the strange horror of its appearance. The peculiar V-shaped mouth with its pointed upper lip, the absence of brow ridges, the absence of chin beneath the wedge-like low lip, the incessant quivering of this mouth, the Gorgon groups of tentacles, the tumultuous breathing of the lungs in a strange atmosphere, the evident heaviness and painfulness of movement due to the

greater gravitational energy of the earth—above all, the extraordinary intensity of the immense eyes—were at one vital,
intense, inhuman, crippled and monstrous. There was something
fungoid in the oily brown skin, something in the clumsy delib-
eration of the tedious movements unspeakably nasty. Even at this
first encounter, this first glimpse, I was overcome with disgust
and hatred. (1898, pp. 21–2)

The reaction of horror, disgust, fear and hatred to the unknown
creature is characteristic. Wells uses the novel to criticise religious
belief in the person of the curate who is completely spineless and
can only think in terms of what the local town of Weybridge has
done to deserve its fate:

"—What has Weybridge done? Everything gone—everything
destroyed. The Church! We rebuilt it only three years ago. Gone!
—swept out of existence! Why?"
    Another pause and he broke out again like one demented.
    "The smoke of her burning goeth up for ever and ever!" He
shouted. (1898, p. 70)

By contrast the character of the Artillery man is made of much sterner
stuff. He is prepared to study the Martians in order to exploit their
weaknesses and if necessary start an underground resistance
movement.

    In the event the Martians are not undone by the assembled wea-
ponry aimed at them by human beings who only succeed in killing
the odd stray Martian. Wells uses a neat Darwinian device to dispose of the enemy. They are crippled and eventually die as a result
of exposure to bacteria that exist on earth but not on Mars. Unlike
humans, they have not built up resistance over the millenia and they
gradually collapse and die.

    The War of the Worlds was a very realistic novel for its time.
Knowledge of the planets was such that it was quite feasible that
aliens of the kind described by Well might exist. However, like
Austen, Wells is not immune to the lure of the "happily ever after
ending". Against all the odds, the narrator is reunited with his wife
at the end of the story, although the novel concludes—the Martians
may yet return . . . "We have learned now that we cannot regard this

planet as being fenced in a secure abiding-place for Man; we can never anticipate the unseen good or evil that may come upon us suddenly out of space." (1898, pp. 178–9) The survival of the fittest— in this case the survival of man—is safe for the time being.

It is fascinating to note the significant changes to the plotting of *The War of the Worlds* in the 2005 screen version starring Tom Cruise as the narrator. The curate and the Artillery man are combined into one character and explicit Darwinian references to the overthrow of the Martians are carefully omitted. Perhaps, in the creationist culture of much of Middle America, religious prejudice means that the original story cannot be allowed to stand. The next chapter will look at the special place of religion in the fantasies of believers and non-believers alike.

CHAPTER SIX

I believe . . .

Religious themes appeared from time to time in the previous chapter but were not the central focus of attention. We will now take a closer look at the part they play in the everyday life of both devout believers and avowed atheists. I will start with a brief clinical vignette.

Deirdre occasionally attends Church. She doesn't go to services regularly but she demands that a priest should exorcise her demons. Deirdre sits in Diana's consulting room crying. She sobs, "Don't talk to me about religion: *(at this point in time, Diana has said nothing).* I went to see Father Denis and said I wanted an exorcism, and he said he didn't want to do it". *There is a pause.* "You don't believe in religion, do you", *she continues,* "that's why you're keeping quiet."

Deirdre's "birth" father Derek is an alcoholic and spends all his wife Dorothy's hard-earned cash. Her younger brother Donny is contemptuous of women in general and his mother and sister in particular. Deirdre speculates, without concrete evidence, that her shadowy older brother Dougal who has long since emigrated may have sexually abused her. It is clear however, that certainly emotional abuse and possibly physical or sexual abuse regularly still take place. At the beginning of the analysis, the source of the abuse, and indeed, whether it is real or imagined, remains vague. Deirdre often comments on the fact that her mother is a doormat, treated like dirt by all the men of the family. Deirdre has a boyfriend, Dan, who turns up to take her out occasionally if he happens to feel like it but who also disappears and cannot be contacted for days on end. The source of his wealth is a profane mystery. Thus, Deirdre both likes men and despises them at the same time. Her previous medical history includes attempted overdoses and episodes of cutting and she is a regular frequenter of the local hospitals. Deirdre accuses her mother Dorothy of being to blame for her misery. She discounts the role of the men in her family, flatly asserting, "This is the way life is—men just behave like this and there's nothing anyone can do about it". Deirdre's opinions about her life, her relationships and her studies—in fact about everything—are expressed as certainties.

Deirdre has an endless list of obsessions. She is worried about remembering to lock the car door when she parks. Has she turned the gas off on the cooker? Will she fail her exams? Has she memorised enough of the course to pass? Will she ever be able to live apart from her parents? Exorcism does not remove these fears, yet Deirdre believes in its powers. As well as occasionally attending church, Deirdre sees her therapist Diana twice a week. Will therapy work where exorcism has failed? Is therapy simply another kind of religion? Will Diana exorcise her demons for her?

Deirdre's story is a complex account with intertwining threads connecting sexual feelings/sexual abuse, unquestioning religious belief/religious questions and a whole series of questions which start with phrases like "Will I, won't I?" and "Have I, haven't I?" This brief summary of some of the issues in Deirdre's story demonstrates that, as in the chapter on negation, the problem of contradictory impulses looms large. For the purposes of this chapter however, I will concentrate on the role of religious belief in Deirdre's story. How does religious belief interact with our anxieties about death and the possibility or otherwise of an afterlife? Is religious belief in some sense a construction of fantasy to ward off anxiety? Even the choice of the religious theme as one among many leaves complex issues for discussion, not least the fact that religious belief can create anxieties as well as relieving them.

What constitutes a religion?

What is the thread that connects the minutely detailed requirements for appropriate religious observance of Orthodox Jewry, the strident call to action, even martyrdom of some fundamentalist Muslim sects, the proselytizing zeal of American fundamentalist Christian movements, the traditional, middle-aged, middlebrow religious practice of the Church of England stalwarts and the "anything goes" philosophy of New Age movements? Religions are often a focal point for groups of people who experience the effects of shared beliefs. Thus, one reading of religion is that it is primarily a group experience but this is complicated because of the interaction of two factors. Firstly, the beliefs of, say, Christians and Hindus clearly produce views about how one should live one's life and what life might mean; some aspects are often similar, but others are markedly different. Secondly, and at the same time, the uniquely individual internal structuring of fantasies that we build up from birth onwards means that even where we closely identify with someone else's belief, it is never identical. It is possible however to look at religion through the other end of the telescope, and study its effects on individuals like Deirdre.

The notion of similarity and difference needs further explanation. During a seminar on Freud a student asked me how one might interpret the word "rose". Rather than tackle this question directly, I asked for the first immediate association to "rose" from each person in the group. The answers I received included the following: "pink", "red", "blood", "love" (twice), "something rising" and "my name means 'rose'". If associations to a single word differ so widely, there is no hope for the notion of identical religious beliefs. On the other hand, from a different perspective, each member of the group had arrived at an individual association to the word using a similar mental process—an association of ideas.

Once again, Freud provides a springboard for starting a discussion of the complex interaction of personal and group religious fantasies. In *Civilization and Its Discontents*, Freud claims that the origin of religious needs is as follows:

The derivation of religious needs from the infant's helplessness and the longing for the father aroused by it seems to be incontrovertible, especially since the feeling is not simply prolonged from childhood days, but is permanently sustained by fear of the superior power of Fate. (Freud, 1930a, p. 72)

It may be obvious that helplessness indeed produces anxiety, but why does Freud link religious needs to the longing for the father? In the spirit of his times, Freud connects the idea of organised religion to the fact that some religions have hierarchies. In a nutshell, Freud asserts that religions need leaders or father figures reflecting the patriarchal view of his day. The contemporary view that "families need fathers" could be seen as an acknowledgment of the need for fathers that neglects the complex issue of whether or not families also need leaders as Paul Verhaeghe persuasively argues in his essay "fathers in flight" in his book, *Love in a Time of Loneliness* (Verhaeghe, 1999, pp. 73–141).

On the other hand, a traditional sociological writer such as Durkheim, places religion in the field of the social rather than the personal.

> . . . [R]eligion is above all a system of notions by which individuals imagine the society to which they belong and their obscure yet intimate relations with that society . . . For it is an eternal truth that something exists outside us that is greater than we are, and with which we commune. (Durkheim, 1912, pp. 70–1)

Using the example of Deirdre, we can see that both Freud and Durkheim may be right. Deirdre has an individualist approach to religion—an exorcism is an avowedly personal experience for the "exorcisee", not a form of collective worship. Yet religion also represents for her a group to whom she can appeal for help. Exorcism is the act of casting "something" out of someone else's mind. It therefore involves more than one person and it usually requires the assent of the group. In Deirdre's case, one of the reasons that Father Denis is not prepared to carry out the exorcism is precisely because he does not have the consent to this action of the religious grouping to which he belongs.

Returning to Freud, we can ask ourselves the next question: why are groups, including religious groups, formed at all? Why isn't religion simply a matter of individual belief? This question is addressed by Freud in *Group Psychology and the Analysis of the Ego*, where he suggests that two forces are at work in the maintenance of a group. They derive from opposite points of the emotional spectrum. The first is as follows and constitutes the "stick" of what we can term the "stick and carrot" approach:

> A Church and an army are artificial groups—that is, a certain external force is employed to prevent them from disintegrating and to check alterations in their structure. As a rule a person is not consulted, or is given no choice, as to whether he wants to enter such a group; any attempt at leaving it is usually met with persecution or with severe punishment, or has quite definite conditions attached to it. (1921c, p. 93)

The second factor, "the carrot", is

> In a Church, . . . as well as in an army . . . the same illusion holds good of there being a head—in the Catholic Church Christ, in an army its Commander-in-Chief—who loves all the individuals with an equal love. Everything depends upon this illusion; if it were to be dropped, then both Church and army would dissolve, so far as the external force permitted them to . . . A democratic strain runs through the Church, for the very reason that before Christ everyone is equal, and that everyone has an equal share in his love. (1921c, pp. 93–4)

This definition fits a wide variety of religious movements of both the traditional and the fundamentalist variety. Yet, Freud's formulation of a religion as an organised system of belief supported by the fantasy of "all men are equal before God" on the one hand, and the image of the patriarchal leader on the other, does not really address the issue of the vast differences between fundamentalist religions at one end of the spectrum and New Age religions at the other. We need to take Freud's definition further; one might legitimately argue that the more "extreme" or "fundamental" the claims of a particular religion, the greater will be the threat of persecution or punishment for leaving and the tighter will be the link between the leader and the led.

* * *

Religions can be broadly divided into four groups, each with distinct characteristics. It might seem that these groups have the arbitrariness of descriptive labels. However, each type of religious belief could also be said to correspond to a particular unconscious psychic structuring of anxiety, producing fantasies that have properties that distinguish them from the prevalent fantasies in another group. Above all, each grouping has a different relationship to that most fundamental of problems for human beings—our future death.

The fundamentalists

Fundamentalist religions demand a high price in return for moral certainties and often, although not always, the assurance of a life after death. The price of certainty is the conviction that everyone else is not only wrong but also damned for even mild-mannered disagreement. It would seem that those who do not share precisely the same beliefs are not just those in the no-man's land densely populated by agnostics, they include those whose beliefs are seen to deviate even slightly from the party line. Fundamentalists believe that non-believers are not simply cast out from their midst, they are condemned to descend into hell; they are also prone to taking an aggressive moral stance even against those who write books that are not meant to have any obvious religious connotation. Currently, J.K. Rowling's Harry Potter books are disapproved of by some conservative American sects despite (or perhaps because of?) the fact that the reader is not seriously expected to believe in sorcery, Quidditch or the existence of Voldemort. Being a fundamentalist can be a time-consuming business. Dealing with non-believers is simple stuff compared to the time and trouble taken with the fine discriminations between one's own religious position and that of one's equally fanatical neighbour—what Freud termed "the narcissism of minor differences" (1918a, p. 199).

What is the price to pay for fundamentalist beliefs? The first casualty is humour. The episode of *The Simpsons* where Homer, Marge and the kids fall asleep in church during the sermon and then have a series of irreverent dreams based on scenes from the Bible is variously, blasphemous to fundamentalists or hilariously funny to less committed couch potatoes.

The second casualty is empathy—the capacity to imagine a situation from another's point of view. Fundamentalists make terrible negotiators because their certainty allows no room for doubt, no space for the possibility of something being different. The political hotspots of the world are dominated by clashes between groups who often share not only much of their cultural heritage and racial origins but also a fundamentalist attitude to religion. Religious differences fuel the fire of nationalism, whether the countries in question are India and Pakistan, the state of Israel or North and South Korea where, in the case of North Korea, politics are infused with quasi-religious zealotry. A striking aspect of fundamentalism is the lack of any reciprocal curiosity. Whilst the West may be shocked, repelled and perhaps even fascinated by the terrible acts of destruction carried out by al-Q'aida, it is extremely doubtful that Osama Bin Laden is particularly interested in the varying reactions of the Western powers. Bernard Lewis makes the following interesting observation on the history of the Middle East:

> . . . [T]he Renaissance, the Reformation, and the technological revolution passed virtually unnoticed in the lands of Islam, where they were still inclined to dismiss the denizens of the lands beyond the Western Frontier as benighted barbarians, much inferior even to the more sophisticated Asian infidels to the east. (2002, p. 8)

The combination of politics with religion suggests a third price that is exacted for fundamentalist beliefs. It is paid by those who dissent or disagree. In order to ward off the possibility of someone, anyone, questioning their certainty of being right, fundamentalists in extreme cases resort to killing, murder and genocide. This is one of several ways of understanding the activities of suicide bombers or the actions of someone like Paul Hill who shot a doctor and his bodyguard, both of whom worked for an abortion clinic in Florida.

As Lewis remarks:

> At the present time, secularism is in a bad way in the Middle East. Of those Middle Eastern states that have written constitutions, only two have no established religion. One is Lebanon, no longer an encouraging example of religious tolerance or secularization.

The other . . . is the Turkish Republic, where, while the general principle of separation [between religion and the state] is maintained, there has been some erosion. (2002, p. 120)

Secularism is not of course the same thing as atheism. A secular state does not allow religious belief to dominate political decision-making; rather it allows individuals to retain their own religious beliefs. Secularism makes a clear distinction between the political and the personal, between religion and culture. Fundamentalism is opposed to this distinction; it wants to make the psychotic move towards accretion and fusion of attitudes so that the political and the personal, religion and culture, are all aligned, all as one.

Fundamentalism has a formulation that is quite simple. If anxiety is to be literally kept out of mind, then the mind has to be filled with the absolute certainty of moral rectitude and a belief in God which cannot be questioned. There is then no space for doubt, that fertile area for imagination, for thinking about life differently for a change. If this analysis in turn seems excessive, it is an interesting exercise to try to name a work of fiction written by a zealot that captures the popular imagination or to find a TV station run by a fundamentalist religious grouping at top of the viewing ratings. Milton's *Paradise Lost* might be the exception that proves the rule, but it can be argued that its wide appeal today is precisely because the arguments and indignation aroused by the concept of the divine rights of kings to rule have now subsided. Its fundamentalism has mutated into poetry with an interesting historical subtext. Indeed, one of the crucial roles played by fantasy in the life of human beings is that it enables perceptions of the world to change.

If anxiety is excluded from the consciousness of fundamentalists, how is it manifested unconsciously in ways that others can spot? In Freud's view, putting something out of mind, not remembering it, inexorably returns in the form of "a compulsion to repeat". (1914g, p. 150) Freud argues that if you repress doubt and fill your mind with certainty, the doubt will not disappear entirely. It will become unconscious and come back to haunt you even if you are unaware of it. Thus, fundamentalists' beliefs are not quite as simple as they look. Their chosen form of religion is a body of certain truths. Anxiety haunts these beliefs and returns in the form of condemning anyone and anything that does not share these certain truths. Indeed, an understanding of the role of anxiety sheds much light on the intolerance of fundamentalists since they literally cannot bear uncertainty. Anything that threatens certainty must be expelled as a noxious substance, a contaminant of the "pure" faith. Missionary zeal is driven by unconscious anxiety—there *must not* be another point of view, another faith or another religion, otherwise . . . the doubts are never spelled out.

To return for a moment to the mind of the individual funda-mentalist believer, there are two very different possibilities. Leaders of sects often have a psychotic structure. As discussed in chapter two, a psychotic *must* believe in his view of the world with absolute certainty. Thus, David Icke is compelled to believe in the role of reptiles in the world order—otherwise he is adrift in a meaningless universe. The followers, however, often have a neurotic structure. Being told what to think is a good method of keeping nagging doubts about the meaning of our lives, death and sexuality all at bay. The simpler the solution, the better it is. *The Hitchhiker's Guide to the Galaxy* meaning of the universe is "forty-two", or, following Keats:

"Beauty is truth, truth beauty, —that is all
  Ye know on earth, and all ye need to know."

Perhaps it is significant that Keats's ode is addressed to a Grecian Urn, that forty-two is a number and reptiles are not people. Does fundamentalism involve removing the human (and often the humane at the same time) from fantasising?

The traditionalists

Traditional religions often preach tolerance, moderation and the middle way. The extremities of the fundamentalist approach to religion are thus to be avoided but not condemned since this in itself would be an extreme attitude to adopt. In other words, much subtle shifting of positions goes on in the area adopted by traditionalists. The Ecumenical movement within Christianity derives its power from the perception that people can negotiate away their differences or "agree to disagree".

The origin of the word "tradition" (and thereby of course "traditionalist") is interesting. According to Raymond Williams, the root word in Latin has the following meanings:

(i) delivery, (ii) handing down knowledge, (iii) passing on a doctrine, (iv) surrender or betrayal. (1976, pp. 318–19)

Williams comments:

When we look at the detailed processes of any of these traditions, indeed when we realise that there are traditions ... and that only some of them or parts of them have been selected for our respect and duty, we can see how difficult tradition really is, in an abstract or exhortatory or, as so often, ratifying use.

It is sometimes observed, by those who have looked into particular traditions that it only takes two generations to make anything traditional: naturally enough, since that is the sense of tradition as active process. But the word tends to move towards age-old and towards ceremony, duty and respect. Considering only how much has been handed down to us, and how various it actually is, this, in its own way, is both a betrayal and surrender. (1976, p. 319)

This statement seems particularly relevant to the attitude of traditionalists to anxiety. The perception that traditional religions often wish to convey is indeed the view that their practice is age-old and handed down. We might then ask, but why should the traditionalist want or need to put across this view of religion?

The answer lies in the opportunity for traditionalists to claim that if something is "age-old" then it has not changed for many years. They go on to make a further claim—that therefore the system of beliefs and concomitant practice of their version of religion must be "correct". The assumption that, simply because something has not changed it must be correct, is one that human beings like very much. It offers the illusory prospect of the security of sameness in an uncertain world. A systematic set of beliefs gives a person a clear structure by and through which they can live their lives with less anxiety.

Compared to fundamentalism, traditional beliefs therefore offer a different but equally effective bulwark against the threat of anxiety.

There is a little more space for manoeuvre since negotiation can take place with other groups occupying the centre ground. The opportunity for thinking outside the framework of the religion is constrained by three factors, the need for the preservation of apparent sameness, the need to occupy the middle ground (in order to distinguish themselves from fundamentalists) and last but not least, the absolute necessity for belief in the religious system of one's choice. Whilst traditionalists may be more flexible than fundamentalists, they are still relatively blinkered by the security of a faith which excludes the apparent danger of "extreme" views. Anxiety is still kept at bay by a system of belief.

Traditionalists often work hard in order to acquire their system of beliefs. People with obsessional traits may find this style of religion of particular appeal. Many happy hours can be spent analysing *precisely* the correct rituals to be followed in the observance of faith and/or in distinguishing the tenets of your own belief from those of your neighbour worshipping in the church next door. An obsessional's work is never done, since the oscillation between one set of ideas and another never ceases. Thus, religious belief and knowledge always remains incomplete and observance of the faith will always leave something further to be desired . . .

The "New Ageists"

There is a group of religious believers who, far from excluding other religions, seek to embrace everyone. Once more however, there is a price to pay. The apparent rise of religious apathy in much of the Western world and the growth of the notoriously fluffy and vague claims of the New Age movements fit into a new kind of picture. Nobody is drummed out of a New Age movement; indeed people often flit from one "belief" to another apparently aimlessly, like butterflies roaming around a garden.

If you watch butterflies carefully, it becomes obvious that their actions are not as random as they might at first appear. Whilst the wind and the rain may make the flight of butterflies seem unpredictable, nevertheless, their behaviour does have reference points that introduce a modicum of determinism or what, in human beings, might be called "rationality".

A given set of rules observed by most religions is not essential for New Age beliefs. What is interesting about them, whether they be about crystals or Ley Lines, is their continuing connection, however tenuous and circumstantial, with the *idea* of belief. The emphasis may be on spiritual cleansing, catharsis and/or a form of spiritual response either to ritual or to natural phenomena. (It is notable that humanistic psychotherapies often conceive of catharsis as one of their principal aims). Many, although by no means all, these therapies have close connections with religions such as "happy-clappy" forms of Christianity that encourage catharsis or, as in the case of the Findhorn Community in Northern Scotland, incorporate spiritual beliefs of some kind into their practice. Sometimes the ritual relics of an older age are reinvented for the purposes of the present day, for example the religious gatherings at Stonehenge during the summer solstice—it is a fair bet that present day druids have very little resemblance to the original druids of prehistoric times.

How do New Ageists grapple with the unavoidable fact that life is haunted by the spectre of death around the corner? The life of the butterfly can shed more light. Butterflies do not deal with their rivals through condemnation or missionary zeal; butterfly does not eat butterfly; butterflies do not plan their short lives; they do not hunt down prey. Butterflies are always in the air; occasionally they alight to drink nectar; even more occasionally they copulate and then the females lay eggs. Most of the time however, butterflies are on the move—they are flying.

New Age beliefs are characterised by their huge variety. There is no necessity for one set of beliefs to be compatible with another. A New Age believer can flit from one practice to another or combine them—aromatherapy, healing crystals, Feng Shui and Reiki today; Ley Lines and tarot cards tomorrow—as the mood takes them. Unlike Freud's "stick" formulation, there is no organised New Age movement with a leader at its head, simply an extremely loose network of ideas characterised by flexibility, response to fashion trends and by the tendency to produce a comforting answer if a question looms which might have an anxiety lurking in its hinterland. New Ageists do not conform to the "carrot" part of Freud's formulation either. All ideas are deemed to be equally valuable and the people who make use of these ideas are neither judged nor are they judgemental. There is no demand for proof of the efficacy of any practice—indeed, a demand for scientific rigour is often one of the few ways to rouse a New Ageist to a state of indignation.

On the face of it, anxiety simply does not figure in the spectrum of New Age beliefs. However, it is still a factor at play. Firstly, fundamental existential anxiety produced by the simple fact that all human beings die is "diluted". It is split up into many much smaller and thus apparently less threatening anxieties or doubts. Each doubt can then be addressed by a tailored individual response. Thus, no two New Age aficionados are likely to believe in the same set of ideas. Each believer will seek his own solution to the problem of dealing with death.

The second solution to the problem of anxiety for New Ageists is their constant need for change, like the butterfly flitting from one buddleia to another. New Age beliefs can be characterised by a lack of rigour. It does not take years to train someone to use crystals, find Ley Lines or read palms because, in truth, there is not very much to learn in the first place! We do not find books offering different approaches to the identification and meaning of tarot cards or a comparison of their efficacy with other methods of prediction. Go to a website on Ley Lines and it will be much more likely to offer you a couple of pages of descriptive information accompanied by some nice photographs and then divert the reader to cup marks, divining rods and electro-stress. The degree of anxiety experienced by New Ageists indeed seems small. However, it is no accident that New Age beliefs are not well equipped to deal with the really serious issues of life and death. In the case of the latter, a New Age belief is often supplanted or supplemented by a sudden recourse to more traditional religions. The local church was suddenly filled with mourners after the horrifying murder of two ten-year-old girls in Soham.

New Age religion, for all its vagueness, occupies the regular slot on Sunday morning television once taken by traditional religious services (the regularity itself is of course a kind of "ritual"). I have in mind shows like the BBC1 *Heaven and Earth Show* typically replete with interviews where celebrities are asked to discuss their personal beliefs, "investigations" of areas on the map where Ley Lines are said to intersect (usually in a picturesque part of the countryside), a suitable recipe for Sunday fare is concocted and so forth. Where once religious fervour was the preserve of a minority of true believers and religious apathy combined with observance of the formal trappings of ritual—the position of the silent majority in Britain—nowadays, the picture is more varied. If religion is broadly defined and is deemed to include New Age beliefs, then it is far from dead. Like the famous conversion symptoms of Freud's hysterics, religious belief is like a chameleon—it changes its shape to suit the demands of its contemporary surroundings. At the turn of the century, the symptoms of Freud's hysterics included facial tics, the smelling of burnt toast, aphonia (inability to speak), and the incapacity to use limbs; nowadays conversion hysteria is still alive and kicking in guises such as anorexia, bulimia, cutting and panic attacks.

New Age beliefs are characterised by extreme flexibility—a natural home for many with a hysterical structure and therefore attractive to people with widely varying attitudes to life. They flourish best in wealthy societies where people can pretend that life is here indefinitely since death is not staring them in the face on the doorstep each day.

The atheists, agnostics and religious objectors

Rejection, like acceptance, can take many forms. Varieties of both belief and unbelief then, come in all shapes and sizes. Considering even those who vehemently reject all religion prompts the question: why does rejection need to be so emotionally charged? There are those who are attracted to the comforts of ritual even if they do not actually "believe" in them—which prompts another interesting question: why do they bother? It is clear that even where formal religious practices were forbidden, as in Soviet Russia for example, societies still provide rituals for marriage and burial of the dead.

If religion is defined as a belief in something, what then, is the status of partial or non-believers whether atheists or agnostics? Formal religious observance has declined steadily in many European countries for the last two centuries and since the Second World War, the rate of decline has accelerated in most of Europe. So how do atheists and agnostics deal with anxiety?

Before we attempt to answer this question it will be helpful to make some more precise distinctions between religious belief, agnosticism and atheism. Although the ethical societies in Britain were a small group, their very smallness enables us to perceive the subtle and varied shifts that a group make in their passage (in this case) from belief to unbelief. In her book, *Varieties of Unbelief: Atheists and Agnostics in British Society 1850–1960* (the title acknowledges her debt to William James), Susan Budd gives an interesting account of the changes that take place when a society shifts from belief to unbelief. She demonstrates that although formal religion and churchgoing in England declined gradually from the beginning of the nineteenth century onwards, its place was not taken by a vacuum but by a "halfway house"—the phenomenon of the ethical movement. In her chapter on the origins of the ethical movement, she comments:

> . . . [T]he extraordinary self-confidence and vitality of many Victorians had its converse in an equally characteristic anxiety and doubt. Their *fears* were many: revolution, cultural anarchy, rampant sexuality and a kind of decay and falling apart of a society in which traditional bonds were daily being eroded and overthrown. (1977, p. 199) (my italics).

The response of the Victorians to these fears is interesting. The ethical movement had all the trappings of a religion—regular meetings, a devotional service including ethical prayers and ethical hymns, and the use of ritual. Budd remarks, "Although we have come to realize the importance of ritual for social life it is a difficult topic to examine, since by definition, its meaning and its effects are most importantly concerned with *that which cannot be put into words*" (1977, p. 215) (my italics).

Today, the ethical movement in turn has been replaced variously by:

(a) The infinitely diverse beliefs of New Ageists;

(b) "Career" atheists who make a fetish out of disbelief leading the sceptical observer to wonder why they are so loud in their claims of unbelief—there is a reminder here of the patient's remark in the earlier chapter on negation when he informs Freud that "it is not about my mother"; and

(c) Many depressed people now frequent the consulting rooms of doctors, psychotherapists, counsellors and the like, when in the past they would have turned to the formal trappings of either of religion or quasi-religions such as the ethical movements.

Religion and the use of ritual

It is clear that even in situations where people ostensibly reject religious beliefs, there is a tendency to cling to their forms and formulae. Fundamentalists, Traditionalists, New Ageists and even agnostics and atheists have a place for ritual, even if not for religion, in their lives. The ethical movement demonstrates a very gradual way in which people can move from unquestioning belief in religion, to unquestioning rejection of religion. Interestingly, the use of ritual remains intact throughout. The distinction between what can be expressed in words and what remains outside language is a crucial one. The border area between an anxiety which cannot be put into words (a trauma) and religion expressed in words and/or music is occupied by ritual. As Budd says:

> The crossing of the boundary is dangerous; it is effected by the use of ritual which sets apart both the occasion and its partici-pants and which makes the crossing irreversible. But in our society, the transition between childhood and adult life, between being single and being married, between being a member of one group and of another, even between being alive and being dead, no longer has this magical, irreversible, final quality. (1977, p. 242)

Ritual, like Freud's definition of a symptom—the two have many similarities—can be understood as a compromise. It enables people to deal with something by substituting ritual/symptom for the orig-inal anxiety. It offers relief, but at the expense of firstly, not "remem-bering" the original cause of the anxiety (Freud considered that it had been repressed) and secondly finding that the ritual/symptom needs to be repeated in order to keep warding off the anxiety. This is another version of the Freudian "compulsion to repeat" referred to earlier in this chapter (1914g, p. 150), although interestingly, Freud does not mention the key role of anxiety in this paper.

Thus, although we *believe* that the crossing of boundaries repre-sented by rituals "no longer has this magical, irreversible, final quality" (Budd, 1977, p. 242), our apparent lack of belief, is not as all-embracing as we might think. One might take the view that the work of Arnold van Gennep (1908) on the importance of the liminal, the delineation of boundaries and the use of *rites de passage* as a means of crossing boundaries in culture, for example, from childhood to adulthood, is unwittingly put into question by New Age phenomena. Yet, the place of magic in our lives has shifted but by no means disappeared. Modern societies are full of instances where rituals are still observed even if power of their original meaning is absent. The custom of marriage is alive and kicking even possibly growing again in popularity. Some newer quasi-religious customs have come into being such as the "memory box" where someone who is dying and/or their relatives collect items to keep in a memory box to remind their loved ones of their life once they have passed away.

Psychoanalytic structure and religious beliefs

Earlier in this chapter, it was suggested that "the *uniquely individual* internal structuring of fantasies that we build up from birth onwards means that even where we closely identify with someone else's belief, it is never identical." If religious fantasies have different underlying structures, then what of the different psychic structures in individual human beings? As the earlier chapter on negative dialectics indicated, Freud proposed a series of distinctions between people based upon the underlying unconscious structure of their largely unconscious fantasies. Lacan's development of these ideas is succinctly summarised by Bruce Fink:

> Thus, the three main diagnostic categories adopted by Lacan are structural categories based on three fundamentally different mechanisms, or what we might call three fundamentally different forms of negation (Verneinung):
>
> | Category | Mechanism |
> |----------|-----------|
> | Neurosis | Repression |
> | Perversion | Disavowal |
> | Psychosis | Foreclosure |
>
> (Fink, 1997, p. 76)

Within the category of neurosis, Freud and Lacan make further distinctions between obsessionality, hysteria and phobia.

It is an intriguing but ultimately fruitless task to attempt to map differing religious beliefs and practices onto different kinds of psychic structure—or vice versa. Although the varieties of negation inherent in religious belief have links to certain structures, it is easy to see glaring exceptions and omissions. Thus, even if most believers in a fervently religious sect have the same psychic structure, (probably a neurotic one), this will not lead to *identical* beliefs and fantasies, because the content and make up of *individual* fantasies is always unique. As I have indicated earlier in the chapter, particular varieties of belief may attract certain kinds of people.

Deirdre has a set of religious beliefs; she has a set of beliefs about her relationship with various family members; she has a set of beliefs about the relationship between herself as an individual and the religious group to which she claims allegiance; and finally she has a set of beliefs about herself. All these beliefs have both conscious and unconscious dimensions and they all operate both intra-psychically and interpsychically. To complicate matters, these structures interact with each other; the *hinges* between structures of religious belief, structures of the internal world of an individual and the external world (relationships between the subject and the other) are all *fantasies*.

Deirdre has a fantasy that exorcism will "fix" the troubling thoughts of possible sexual abuse in her mind. This fantasy is linked to other fantasies about the ability of religious belief to change her perceptions of her relationships with her family. Her obsessional thoughts, repeatedly locking and unlocking the car door for example, are linked to fantasies of perfection and completion—we might even fantasise that they represent unconscious visions of heaven, hell and death. There are, of course, many more fantasies that interconnect in her life—one of many reasons why the exploration of fantasy through psychoanalysis often takes some time.

Groups of fantasies interact with other groups of fantasies, thus accounting for the infinite variety of fantasy and religious belief. Yet overall, there are general similarities between individuals, family groups, regional and even national identities, since fantasies are formed from the common experience of being human, namely, being aware both of our aliveness and the inevitable fact of death ahead of us. Deirdre finds these thoughts difficult to bear, so difficult in fact, that she would like someone to exorcise them.

Safety and unsafety

In the subheading above, I have used "Unsafety" as a noun to draw attention to a more precise contradiction than would be denoted by the use of a word such as "danger". In each case, religion or its absence is a response to anxiety, particularly the fundamental anxiety about the brevity and unpredictability of human life. Whichever way we twist and turn, anxiety remains, just as the certainty of our eventual demise remains. The collective experience of belonging to a religious grouping equates to a collective response to the feelings of safety or unsafety within the group. "Unsafety" is the dominant mode of our existence.

When we feel unsafe, we become anxious and, as Freud and later writers on the topic of anxiety have shown, if we feel *really* unsafe, then our minds may respond by cutting off all memories of anxiety. During the First World War, men in the trenches lived in filthy conditions, endured a relentless repetition of shell shock and saw soldiers dying all round them. Many had a nervous breakdown and were literally unable to carry on fighting. The danger was so great that the breakdown enabled them to "switch off" their memories. Consequently, they could not consciously remember just how unsafe they were. Yet traumatic symptoms such as nightmares, night sweats, inability to move or do anything at all, continued—often for many months and years. The symptoms replaced the memories. Amnesia, lack of memory in the case of extreme anxiety, therefore serves a useful purpose. It places a limit on our experience of trauma. Freud's view was that the cure for trauma lay in gradually persuading sufferers to put into words their unspeakable experiences—one of the tasks of an analysis. The words used to describe horrific events will be different in each individual case—a kind of tailor-made fantasy. The work of the analyst in some circumstances may be to encourage the sufferer to expand these fantasies so that more and more symptoms (representations of forgotten experiences through actions or apparently illogical thoughts and fears) are replaced with words that connect in a more "truthful" way with the patient's experience.

Returning to Deirdre, the analyst Diana's task is a delicate one—to pick a way through the thicket of Deirdre's intertwined desires, fantasies and traumas. Diana has to facilitate Deirdre's thinking about some of her fantasies that are, on the face of things, too painful to consider, and to allow Deirdre to construct a new set of relationships between her internal thoughts and the external realities of her world. These new relationships will also be fantasies—what else do human beings have as a means of describing and explaining their experience? Both Diana and Deirdre also hope that her changed experience of her life will result in diminished anxiety. Gradually, over many months, the external facts of Deirdre's life change dramatically. Deirdre succeeds in coming more punctually to analysis because she no longer spends time checking the gas tap on the cooker and locking and unlocking the car door. She ditches her boyfriend, passes her exams and uses her new qualification to find paid work for the first time. However, although Diana and Deirdre spend some time talking about these external issues, during the analysis Diana listens to an extended and detailed account of Deirdre's sexual and religious fantasies as they slowly come to light. To begin with, Deirdre blames her father Derek for everything that is wrong in her life. Then her target shifts to her mother Dorothy the hardworking doormat. Later and with great difficulty amidst many tears, Deirdre remembers a series of humiliating sexual rituals that her older brother Dougal forced her to endure. The role of religion in Deirdre's life shifts from centre stage to the periphery.

The role of doubt (whether or not interwoven with religious fantasy) constitutes an important feature of an analysis. Doubt produces new material as follows: the analysand can never be sure what it is that the analyst wants since the analyst refuses to answer direct questions of this kind. The corollary is that what the analyst "wants" is to promote doubt in the mind of the analysand, which leads to more questions . . . In Deirdre's case, the role of the analyst, Diana, is to question the certainties in her initial story and help Deirdre to shed doubt over them.

Sometimes there are no questions. Amnesia is an extreme form of coping with extreme anxiety where symptoms without apparent language components replace fantasy. In less extreme situations, fantasies, including of course religious fantasies, are the means through which feelings of unsafety are kept at bay. Part of the protective value of both symptoms and fantasies is that they are "unaccountable"— difficult to put into words. In Deirdre's case, Diana may never know whether abuse took place and was then forgotten as a means of defence or whether the abuse was imagined as a means of defence to replace even more unbearable and unacceptable (to Deirdre) incestuous feelings of sexual attraction as well as repulsion towards Dougal. It is of course possible that both of these conjectures are correct.

If unsafety is "unaccountable", we might then expect that its opposite, feelings of safety, might be easier for someone to explain and put into words. Yet, in his classic study of religion, *Varieties of Religious Belief*, William James shows that this is not the case. Here is a quotation from an individual, but nonetheless typical, religious experience:

> "A paradise of inward tranquillity" seems to be faith's usual result; and it is easy, even without being religious one's self, to understand this. . . . *in treating of the sense of God's presence, I spoke of the unaccountable feeling of safety which one may then have.* And, indeed, how can it possibly fail to steady the nerves, to cool the fever, and appease the fret, if one be sensibly conscious that, no matter what one's difficulties for the moment may appear to be, one's life as a whole is in the keeping of a power whom one can absolutely trust? In deeply religious men the abandonment of self to this power is passionate. Whoever not only says, but *feels*, "God's will be done," is mailed against every weakness; and the whole historic array of martyrs, missionaries, and religious reformers is there to prove the tranquil-mindedness, under naturally agitating or distressing circumstances, which self-surrender brings. (1902, p. 285) (first set of italics are mine)

I have quoted at some length to convey the flavour of James' approach to his project, since it is an extended and sometimes amusing treatise on the uses to which religion is put by human beings. He describes very well the complex relationship between an individual and his God. James highlights the feeling of security that is generated as a result of believing; but why is it that the feeling of *safety* is "unaccountable"—indescribable?

The "unaccountable feeling of safety" could simply mean something mysterious but rather James is referring to a range of feelings often associated with the religiously inflected word—ineffable. We are still left wondering what the "thing" is that is "unaccountable" and ineffable. After all, it is apparently absolutely unthreatening to be safe! It is worth trying to be very precise about these terms. When we feel safe, we are often unaware of this fact. We simply carry on living in the blithe assumption, that, whatever we are doing, all will be well. Of course, disaster can strike at any moment. Death often arrives unexpectedly. The closeness of death is a fact that we try to ignore whenever it is humanly possible.

With James, I am suggesting that our perception of external reality is distorted by religion in order to keep anxiety away. Belief provides relief from the uncertainties and anxieties of existential questions such as wondering why we are here, why does the world exist and so forth. This observation is also true of the role that all religions play in the life of human beings. They offer a "safe" explanation to ward off our anxiety that, in truth, life is meaningless. Ultimately the world is a chaotic and arbitrary place where people, in theory, would prefer that there be order and reason. Many religions offer the prospect of another life after the present one. This proposition not only gives meaning to the present life—often this "meaning" takes the form of a preparation for the next one—but it also offers the prospect of warding of the uncomfortable idea that death is the end of human life, indeed, "the bourn from which no man returns". In the richest countries of the world, we have much more control over our lives than in the past but still as Shakespeare would have it, "Golden lads and girls all must, as chimney sweepers, come to dust." Safety is, therefore, another illusion, maintained by the fantasy that "safety", like the advertisement for varnish where the advertiser reassures his audience that his brand "does just what it says on the tin".

The issue of safety is not only the province of religion. Its effects in the scientific domain are far reaching. As indicated previously and explored in more detail in the next chapter, psychoanalysis avoids the apparent certainties produced by the labels of manuals such as *DSMIV-TR, The Diagnostic and Statistical Manual of Mental Disorders.* If patients' feelings of safety and unsafety are either incapable of being put into words or only with extreme difficulty, then by the same token, they cannot be labelled in any simple way. The Freudian hypothesis employed here rather proposes that neurotics, psychotics and perverts both consciously and unconsciously relate to the world around them in profoundly different ways. As indicated in chapter two, the distinctions are largely concerned with differences in *internal unconscious psychic structure*, not necessarily by any instantly perceptible differences in *external behaviour* (the type of identification relied upon in *DSM-IV*). Thus one can draw some conclusions about the kinds of religions which attract people with different psychic structures.

The majority of religions have a patriarchal structure; men officiate, men decide on the rules. One of the reasons adduced for this is the fact that men are deemed to be unconsciously envious of women—only women can bear children, and until very recent advances in DNA testing, only women could be entirely sure that they are the parent of the children that they bear. Controlling the lives of women using (*inter alia*) religious beliefs and structures, can thus be seen as an attempt to nullify the one inborn certainty that mothers possess compared to men. This has been theorised in many ways, one of the most vivid accounts being that of Dorothy Dinnerstein:

> The dirty goddess is dirty not simply because the flesh that she represents is the vehicle-saboteur of our wishes . . . She is dirty also, more deeply dirty, for another reason: the positive side of what she embodies—our old joy in the flesh and the capacity we still have to feel the kind of contact with life that the flesh originally carried . . . (1976, p. 147).

It is interesting that this account describes a woman as a goddess. Amongst contemporary psychoanalysts, Estela Welldon discusses the close relationship between men's view of women in mothering roles as an idealised madonna or despised whore (Welldon, 1988). In the past, pregnancy was often regarded as a mysterious phenomenon since there is the long delay between conception and birth. Furthermore, until very recently, a father could never been entirely sure of his paternity unless extreme measures were employed such as, in mediaeval times, the wearing of chastity belts. Even in ostensibly less patriarchal times in Western society, control in many spheres is predominantly exercised by men and the focus of their attention is on controlling women and children. Religious dominance is one way of imposing certainties in an uncertain world. The patent unease of many branches of Christian religion with the acceptance of women priests is surely bound up with unconscious fears of what will happen if their sex (here subtly confused with sexuality) is allowed a prominent role in religious practice.

Religious beliefs protect us from the idea that death is final. Even those who have no belief are often superstitious. Very few people can really bear to think that death is inevitable and that perhaps all life is futile and meaningless. Religious certainty is one solution and amnesia is another. The greater the anxiety, then the greater will be the certainty required of the fantasy/religious belief; alternatively, the more comprehensive will be the amnesia, the "forgetting" or "rejection" of other points of view. When anxiety is at a low level, then New Age religions can prosper. If this formulation is correct, then we would expect to find fundamentalist approaches to religion flourishing in those countries where threats to life and limb are endemic. One might then be surprised at the flourishing fundamentalism of the American "bible belt". Here Michael Moore provides an answer in both *Bowling for Columbine* and *Fahrenheit 9–11*. The American gun culture is fuelled by an imagined fear of attack, quite out of proportion to its statistical likelihood and similarly, Moore's analysis of the Bush administration depicts how it plays on the public's fear of attack.

High levels of anxiety drive away the varied responses to life that are engendered by fantasy and encourage either the practice of a religion where certainties replace fantasies or amnesia as a response to trauma. New Age religions often embrace magic and superstition. "Real" religions often dismiss New Ageists perhaps overlooking the fact that belief in magic and superstition is an effective method of dealing with anxiety. The decline in the popularity of witchcraft at the expense of New Age religions was not brought about by an absence of belief, but rather by its replacement with the apparently superior explanations for natural phenomena and misfortunes produced by the scientific explanations of the Age of Reason and its successors (Thomas, 1991).

Not all religions are connected to ideas of an afterlife, but many are. The concept of an afterlife probably originates with the human being's fear of death. Human beings are probably the only species who know that they will die, so the idea of another world offers an attractive solution to a terrifying problem. It is easy then to see how feelings of guilt, vengeance, and propositions such as the existence of an intrinsic meaning in life, can lead to parallel convictions—we will pay in the next life for our behaviour in this and our enemies will meet their just deserts in the life hereafter.

Religious beliefs, of whatever variety, do not come without trappings. Why does religion always seem to be accompanied by a system of ethics and moralising attitudes often interwoven with mysticism? Why indeed, are religion and morality deemed to go together, like that example from another, closely related area of fantasy, "love and marriage"? We could hypothesise that forms of religion that are deemed to be "extreme", usually co-exist with equally extreme attitudes towards morality and the living of a moral life. To quote from another of James's superb examples:

> When you stop at one thing, you cease to open yourself to the All.
>
> For to come to the All you must give up the All.
>
> And if you should attain to owning the All, you must own it, desiring Nothing.
>
> In this spoliation, the soul finds its tranquillity and rest. Profoundly established in the centre of its own nothingness, it can be assailed by naught that comes from below; and since it no longer desires anything, what comes from above cannot depress it; for its desires alone are the causes of its woes (1902, p. 306). [Here James is citing the work of Saint Jean de la Croix, *Vie et Oeuvres*, Paris, 1893, ii.94, 99 abridged].

This is an example of what he describes as "that vertigo of self-contradiction which is so dear to mysticism" (James, 1902, p. 306). Another aspect of this quotation is striking—the use of the phrase, "the All". The notion of contradiction is combined with another characteristic of mysticism, the use of all-embracing omnipotent terms. The question a sceptic might ask is: If one wants to "come to the All", what *exactly* is the "it" that must be given up? To treat the question literally for a moment—to give up everything would mean starving oneself to death by giving up eating and drinking. The same sceptic could then observe that one of the side effects of starvation is hallucination. A sceptical conclusion can thus be drawn, that submitting ourselves to extreme deprivation in the name of religious experience is simply a means of inducing hallucination, another brand of fantasy. It is interesting that, once again, issues of the relationship between certainty, equated here with "the All" and omnipotence are highlighted. A familiar factor also hoves into view here—the role of contradiction. "Safety" and "unsafety" form a contradictory pairing, as do "all" and "nothing". Once again, we are in the territory of the complex interaction of different species of contradiction and negation explored earlier in chapter one, "Variations on a theme of negation".

Conclusion

It is now possible to propose connections between Deirdre's conflicting attitudes towards her brother Dougal's sexual advances, her obsessions and her desire for exorcism. Following the theme of the chapter on negation, with regard to her brother, Deirdre is oscillating between feelings of sexual attraction and repulsion. These feelings are unconscious at the beginning of analysis, only emerging later and in a partial form. Her unconscious conflict is then transferred to other common situations in her life where there is a clear-cut decision to be made—should the gas be turned on or off—should she check the handbrake one more time? When the uncertainty/ unsafety/inability to make a decision becomes unbearable, then in the past she has resorted to cutting herself and suicide attempts, in other words, attempting to produce a final resolution to her unbearable inner conflict. At the beginning of analysis she exchanged these extreme solutions for the less damaging one of exorcism. Deirdre's fantasy is that exorcism will end her endless anxieties. Diana's task is to help Deirdre find a solution that will allow her to bear a modicum of uncertainty instead of dealing with absolutes with potentially fatal consequences such as suicide.

Uncertainty is the key. Where we have superior explanations for catastrophic events, whether they account for droughts or for the death of a child, religious explanations tend to wither away. They flourish in areas, and among people, where life is uncertain. Yet, even in the most secure of societies, the exact hour and precise nature of our deaths is nearly always unknown and a belief of a supernatural kind may help us cope with our inner uncertainties. Negative dialectics operate in the field of religious belief, as elsewhere, via an interesting paradox. As my friend Susan Budd once remarked, "unsafety", doubt and the unknown all continually contribute to our attribution of supernatural powers to other people, things or "spirits"; this is the very stuff of religious belief and the source of Deirdre's initial reliance on exorcism. However, a classical psycho-analytic approach to relieving anxiety is to increase doubt where patients experience emotionally crippling certainties. This may increase anxiety in the short term, but, in the long term, it may offer the only hope of relief from our emotional pain. Thus, a by-product of psychoanalysis is often a lessening of religious fervour. Psycho-analysis and religion both deal in human doubt even if the consequences of these dealings may lead in different directions.

CHAPTER SEVEN

The meaning of fantasy and anxiety

Thus far, the account of the overlap of fantasy and anxiety has pro-
ceeded by viewing them as Siamese twins, joined at the hip,
ostensibly "thinking" separately but nevertheless unable to escape
each other and influencing each other's every move. The story of
these twins has examined the role of dialectics, the function of the
plot and some of the key themes of its content such as religion, gothic
and other tales; an attempt, too, has been made to define anxiety,
the apparently less loved twin. An attentive reader might now ask,
"since the fate of these two modes of being are bound together, with
a plot line and a story, does this story mean anything?" As the chapter
on negative dialectics showed, in the life of the neurotic, dialectical
dilemmas that involve oscillating fantasies and anxiety states are
impossible to escape. The perverse and psychotic states of being
produce avoidances or denials but cannot banish either fantasy or
anxiety. In the process however, they produce a series of outcomes—
meanings, symptoms that are "meaningless" in themselves but
which can take up an enormous amount time and at worst preoccupy
the sufferer completely, or produce stoppages of meaning, otherwise
known as trauma. John Forrester offers a clear account of Freud's
views on this matter:

> In Freud's writings, such a reference, indicating the insertion from
> "outside", is signalled by the use of the prefix "Ur-", translated
> in English as primal. Whether it is the primal father, the primal
> horde, primal words, primal repression, the primal language, the

primal scene, *Urgeschichte*—whichever it is, we are aware that a stop has been put to the sliding of meaning that continually threatens to erupt from the unconscious. The uninhibited sliding is celebrated in schizophrenia, a condition whose name has an etymology which tells exactly the opposite of what it is: a collapse of the separate levels of meaning and reality that constitute the essence of sanity. (Forrester, 1980, p. 130)

This quotation also sheds light on the problems encountered in the second chapter, where psychosis and perversion are posited as conditions where the prospects for fantasy are severely curtailed. As Forrester indicates, sliding never stops in psychosis and meaning has no chance to take hold. In the case of perversion, I suggest that the twins, fantasy and anxiety, are wrapped around each other in such a close embrace that all meaning remains self-referential; it does not slide but constantly circles round like greyhounds chasing the hare on a dog track.

Returning to the neurotic "sliding of meaning that continually threatens to erupt from the unconscious", meaning may be punctuated by facts, and fantasy may be punctuated by anxiety—but can they be separated? The two clearly come together in the following quotation from Ibsen's *Ghosts*:

> MRS ALVING: Ghostlike. When I heard Regina and Oswald in there, it was as if I saw ghosts. I almost think we are all ghosts— all of us. Pastor Manders. It isn't just what we have inherited from our father and mother that walks in us. It is all kinds of dead ideas and all sorts of old and obsolete beliefs. They are not alive in us; but they remain in us none the less, and we can never rid ourselves of them. I've only to take a newspaper and read it, and I see ghosts between the lines. There must be ghosts all over the country. They lie as thick as grains of sand. And we're all so horribly afraid of the light. (Ibsen, 1881, p. 62)

In an earlier chapter, it was argued that one of the functions of gothic fantasies such as *Dracula* was the apparently paradoxical symbolisation of life in death. This extract from Ibsen's *Ghosts*, shows that syphilis (one of the unnamed "ghosts" of the play that has infected many of the characters) can be understood as a disease embodying the role of "*Dracula*" and retaining this apparent paradox. The "dead ideas and old dead beliefs" of the quotation are "not actually alive in us, but they're rooted there all the same, and we can't rid ourselves of them". Life continues in the midst of death and dying via transmission of a deadly infection to the next generation. The sexual mores of the 1880s are at one and the same time both dead in the water and alive and kicking in terms of their continuing effects throughout the play. A careful reading might suggest that Oswald has already unintentionally passed on the disease to a third generation as a result of his unwittingly incestuous affair with his half-sister, Regina the maid.

The original Norwegian title of *Ghosts*, "*Gengangere*" means something similar to the French word "*revenants*". It indicates both the persistent returning of life in the midst of death, and its opposite, the persistent returning of death in the midst of living, rather than simply the residual effects of life after death more obviously denoted by the term "ghosts". Ibsen's publisher anticipated that the work would be a bestseller in view of the worldwide reputation of the playwright and it created a furore when it was originally published —a sure indication that thousands of people thought there was something meaningful going on. (However, unlike today, notoriety meant that the publisher was landed with ten thousand unsold copies!) Syphilis was the Aids of the nineteenth century, a disease whose very name spelled a protracted but nevertheless certain journey towards death and suffering. It also encompassed the distinctly Freudian possibility of the sins of the fathers being unwittingly visited via their wives upon their sons and daughters.

Ghosts dramatizes the consequences of these sins, depicting not only the effect of syphilis on Oswald's brain but the social hypocrisies variously enacted through all the characters in the play. The meaning of the play is located neither simply in the plot nor in its contents as such. Ghosts, "*Gengangere*" are created by a subtle combination of three attributes; firstly, a real organic disease of the body—syphilis, secondly, the "real" anxieties of each of the characters and thirdly, their concomitant fantasies. Each attribute has an ongoing role in the creation of the other two. Several characters in the play make attempts to discount or remove each one of these attributes; but whatever has been taken away does not disappear completely, it becomes repressed, unconscious, slowly gathering power for an explosion like a pressure cooker boiling with a blocked valve. A fourth attribute is also at work here—the question of time. The play is a slowly ticking time bomb of meanings still relevant in the twenty-first century. The revelations in the play never fail to shock even the most sophisticated and hardboiled of audiences. *Ghosts* is the embodiment on stage of a key theme in Freud's writing from *Studies in Hysteria* onwards. As both Freud and Ibsen knew only too well, the repressed has a habit of returning with devastating effects. The potential for devastation is so great that we use both fantasy and anxiety to fend off this knowledge from consciousness. Our "knowledge" is repressed; at the same time relief from some of the pressure engendered by repression is obtained by developing symptoms such as Miss Lucy R's "smell of burnt pudding" (Freud, 1895d, p. 107). In Miss Lucy R's case, she had an unrequited and hopeless love for her employer that she did not dare express consciously and openly—as Mrs Alving might have remarked, she was "horribly afraid of the light". The phantom smell replaced her thoughts about love. Freud concludes:

> It turns out to be a *sine qua non* for the acquisition of hysteria that an incompatibility should develop between the ego and some idea presented to it. . . . The hysterical method of defence . . . lies in the conversion of the excitation into a somatic innervation; and the advantage of this is that the incompatible idea is *repressed* from the ego's consciousness. (Freud, 1895, p. 122 my italics)

At the beginning of this chapter, we put forward the proposition that meaning is established by a combination of three factors, the body, anxiety and fantasy; it is then carried forwards and backwards by time. Using the Freudian tool of investigation by means of exploration of the margins of consciousness, we shall take a closer look by observing what happens when one of these factors is made to take a back seat. Repressing ideas from consciousness does not simply happen in Freud's case studies of hysterical women. Those who put forward theories about anxiety and fantasy also have a tendency to repress uncomfortable facts, resulting in interesting distortions and effects. One of the common tactics employed in different circumstances with similar results is to attempt to conflate fantasy with anxiety.

The first example is a comment on the distinction between empirical and non-empirical research, epitomized as "fantasies don't matter; together with anxiety they can be collapsed into feelings and behaviour and they're all part of the same thing." The second is an observation on the reluctance of human beings to accept that Copernicus is correct—in other words we assume for most practical purposes that we are the centre of the universe, not an insignificant blip in space and time. The third is an attempt to situate the placebo effect in relation to fantasy and anxiety—"anxieties are dispensable". The chapter will then move on to look at the role of time in the process of producing meaning by briefly revisiting Freud's concept of *Nachträglichkeit*. Finally, we will discuss the way in which meaning remains the "ghost in the machine". Meaning is, in many senses, the traces left after the unconscious has been at work on the problems of consciousness, just as fantasy is a series of red herrings, constantly leading us away in all directions from the far-reaching and ever present threat of anxiety.

"Fantasies and anxiety are all part of the same thing"

Are human beings simply very sophisticated machines? In due course, will we be able to elide the distinction between the brain that provides the "hardware" for human actions and the mind that provides the "software"? Even if we were to go down this route, there are numerous opportunities to explore general as opposed to more specific questions. Following Damasio's description of the experience of emotions and feelings in the brain as a tree that operates functionally from roots to twigs and leaves with the trunk and branches as parts of the whole, we do not necessarily have to wait for the findings of molecular biology genetics and evolutionary psychology before we ask questions about how the whole tree operates. Changing the metaphor, we do not have to know how a car works in order to drive one from London to Brighton or, for that matter, from London to Istanbul. Questions about the nature and purpose of the journey itself are only indirectly related to the nature of the vehicle. Our bodies need to exist in order for us to live but the purpose (or lack of it) in being alive in the first place is a different issue.

It is very tempting to follow a writer such as Richard Dawkins down the route that imagination and fantasy are simply by-products of the human brain. In this account, anxiety is simply a useful genetically acquired attribute and fantasy is a meme—an accidental cultural by-product of the process of becoming a human being. He defines his concept of "memes" as follows:

> But do we have to go to distant worlds to find other kinds of replicator and other, consequent, kinds of evolution? I think that a new kind of replicator has emerged on this very planet . . .
>
> The new soup is the soup of human culture. We need a name for the new replicator, a noun that conveys the idea of a unit of cultural transmission, or a unit of imitation. "Mimeme" comes from a suitable Greek root, but I want a monosyllable that sounds a bit like "gene". . . .
>
> Examples of memes are tunes, ideas, catch-phrases, clothes, fashions, ways of making pots of or building arches. . . . If a scientist hears or reads about a good idea, he passes it on to his colleagues and students. He mentions it in his articles and lectures. If the idea catches on, it can be said to propagate itself, spreading from brain to brain. (Dawkins, 1976, p. 192)

In his endnote elaborating this definition, Dawkins remarks that he is "anxious to repeat that his designs on human culture were modest almost to vanishing point" (Dawkins, 1976, p. 322). However, the book as a whole is notable for the assertions that principles of replication combined with Darwinian natural selection govern everything. Perhaps they do. However, Dawkins ignores the importance of language in this argument. The second group of examples of memes are notable for their inclusion of language. As I have argued in this book, some kind of language is essential for the purposes not only of communication but for the experience of both suffering and pleasure. Language operates as a hinge connecting fantasy to anxiety—it is precisely at the point where the Siamese twins, fantasy and anxiety, join at the hip. Dawkins's description is interesting for several reasons. Firstly, uncharacteristically for a writer preoccupied with the detail of how life works—a meme is simply a catch-all descriptive term for cultural examples of fantasy. Dawkins does not explain *why* we should use these terms or what purpose they serve. In his account, genes were doing quite well on their own before memes came along and speeded up the whole process of evolution.

Secondly, the links that cry out to be made between anxiety and fantasy are left untouched. Indeed the differentiated nature of culture is much more clearly expressed using a psychoanalytic account that interrogates the relationship between fantasy and anxiety than a Darwinian one that lumps everything that is not a gene into a melting pot labelled "memes". Differentiation, the task of establishing differences, is a task that language carries out supremely well.

Perhaps Dawkins has some unease about the tendency of his views to offer a new species of "*Weltanshauung*" where the meanings people give to their lives are drawn into a black hole labelled "memes". He cautiously welcomes the work of writers such as Dennett and Humphrey who occupy an intermediate space between the "Fantasies do not matter" position and the opposite extreme represented by proponents of New Age fantasies discussed earlier, where fantasy replaces the need for serious intellectual thought. The proponents of the intermediate stages are not arguing for the disposal of rationalism and logic: rather they try to offer a view of the world that accommodates fantasy. For such writers, all is not yet lost for the largely measurement-free fantasy world of human beings, even if Dawkins, and his colleagues are right about the technicalities of the hard wiring of the brain. *The Mind's I* is a collection of essays on this theme that is now over twenty-five years old. The arguments, however, are still fresh. Here is Nicholas Humphrey's conclusion to his closely argued book on consciousness:

> Looking from my window at this moment I can see the sun setting over the western horizon. In the tradition of my ancestors I am representing the light arriving at my retina both as a circular patch of redness happening to me and as a fiery orb existing in the galaxy out there. But something else has followed in the course of evolution: the seeming miracle of consciousness. I am now living in the present tense of the sensations that "I" bring into being. I am encapsulating my own response to the sun's image as an activity of which "I" am the author. I have, as it were, taken a loop out of the thin rope of physical time, lassoed the sun— and made it, momentarily, mine. (Humphrey, 1992, p. 227)

To be optimistic about brains for a moment, gene therapy research might eventually be directed towards enabling us to be more imaginative and more alive to the possibilities as well as to the dangers of the world around us and not solely preoccupied with trying to correct faults in brain function. Humphrey's argument comes down on the side of sensation being essentially the experience of our internal world and perception being our understanding of the world around us. Thus, contrary to Cartesian theory of *res cogitans* (thinking thing, i.e. mind*)* and *res extensa* (extended thing i.e. body), the body is not split from mind but rather mind operates through two routes that lead to and from the body. These routes cannot be separated; they are intertwined throughout the journey that is life. By extension (but not of the kind intended by Descartes) the unconscious relies on its conscious counterpart to make itself felt and *vice versa*. Sometimes, fantasies will be uppermost and at other times anxiety will attempt to blot out fantasy; each may or may not be unconscious, conscious, or partially conscious at any given time. Since the Cartesian division of those who favour the path of research into effects—what can be seen, heard and measured—and those who try to describe experience "on the hoof", separation of meaning into two categories has often followed. Here is an example of how we experience this apparently paradoxical separation/non-separation in practice.

Imagine you are a visitor to the French chateau of Chambord. You will find two splendid intertwining spiral staircases. As you ascend one, ask a friend to climb the other at the same time. Theoretically, you know that your paths will never cross; intuitively however, as you constantly face each other, so close, yet so far away, you think that you will find yourself on the same staircase as your friend. In reality, you will only meet again at the top. In reality also, the experiences of you and your friend are very similar, but not precisely identical. The *differences* in experience can be measured in some respects since the staircases and your bodies are in measurably different locations. The *similarity* of the experiences cannot be so readily measured in the same way. Psychoanalysis is a discipline that is able to give an account of the phenomenon that encompasses similarity and difference, both conscious and unconscious, at one and the same time. However, since paradox is an essential element in the thought processes of normal human beings, both psychoanalysis and its close relative in this regard, contemporary philosophy, constantly *themselves* fall victim to the effects that they describe so well—the oscillating beliefs and negative dialectics encountered in the first chapter.

A related example to that of Dawkins is the temptation by many philosophers and psychologists to collapse brain and mind together. So far as fantasy and anxiety is concerned, this has the same effect, that of removing any tools for discrimination between the two, let alone between one species of fantasy or anxiety and another. Those who would keep the distinction are not however, always sympathetic to the arguments in this book. There are many who insist on trying to keep minds in the picture even if this means flying in the face of logic. A typical example is the topic of creationism or as it is euphemistically termed "intelligent design". As Dawkins and Coyne, critics of this view, succinctly put it,

> So why are we so sure that intelligent design (ID) is not a real scientific theory, worthy of "both sides" [of the argument] treatment? . . .
> If ID really were a scientific theory, positive evidence for it, gathered through research would fill peer-reviewed scientific journals. This doesn't happen. It isn't that editors refuse to publish ID research. There simply isn't any ID research to publish. (2005, p. 5)

This argument is sound in itself. What is *not* addressed here (and to be fair, this is not the aim of their article) are the *reasons* why ID appeals in the first instance to so many non-scientists and some very powerful political lobbies. The reader of this book might suspect that we are confronted again with the preference of human beings for reassuring fantasies about our origins rather than facing the anxiety arising from the conviction of our certain (and total) death implied in evolutionary theory. As Freud and others have remarked, this view deals a narcissistic wound to our wish for importance and eternity. This point leads me on to my second argument in relation to the connection of fantasy and anxiety.

Wishing that Copernicus were wrong

Fantasy can be seen as an ever-present construction in any human society. In the above example, taken to "the ID extreme", it enables us to pretend that indeed life has a meaning that has somehow been created specially for us. This is a position close to my next argument. We like to believe that we are at the centre of the universe, yet the implication of Copernicus' work is that we live on a small not very significant planet; Darwin came along and demonstrated that we are simply apes, not a race of higher beings. Freud dealt a third blow to our already diminished sense of security and self-importance by suggesting that we are not masters of our own house; we find ourselves constantly doing things in life that we are unable to account for intellectually and rationally. According to him, whether we like it or not, the unconscious has its say.

The French psychoanalyst, Laplanche, elegantly illustrates this phenomenon in his essay entitled, "The incomplete Copernican revolution". He observes that, logically, we "know" that Copernicus is correct, but *actually*, we all behave much of the time as if Copernicus were wrong. We put ourselves at the centre of our own universe. We wake up in the morning and think we can decide what tasks we are going to accomplish. We plan our day. At the end of the day, we have often found ourselves inexplicably deflected from some and perhaps even all of our projected tasks!

Here is an everyday example. In any university the stated intentions of most students are that (a) they will hand in their essays on time and (b) that they will carry out the necessary reading and drafting of their work well before the deadline. In reality, many defer their work until the last possible moment, all the while muttering to those around them the numerous "reasons" for their procrastination. Each "reason" is usually centred around a view of the universe seen from an individual perspective—our computer crashed, the book we wanted wasn't in the library, we "had to" join our friends clubbing at the weekend and couldn't get up on Monday morning, and so on. This account seems normal to most of us but why should this be so? Why should human beings put so much effort into constantly pretending that Copernicus is wrong? We convince ourselves erroneously that we are in charge of our lives but, in fact, we are constantly distracted or led astray by the whims and fantasies of the moment. These are not thoughts that we can easily measure. It may be that some students are more disciplined than others, and therefore *either*, less susceptible to the influence of fantasy and anxiety—they are too busy having fun to care about writing essays *or*, they are overwhelmed by anxiety-provoking fantasies of failure and unable to write. To some degree, the marks that students receive for their essays reflect their ability to analyse facts and their ability to acquire knowledge but they may also provide a clue pointing to the extent to which fantasies and anxieties influence their lives. What is *not* measured by the assessment process is a student's unique and individual experience of fantasy and anxiety or the degree to which she or he is in the grip of conflicting fantasies and anxieties. Students' brains "know" what is required in order to write and essay; their minds also "know" this too but often have other ideas.

Incidentally this mode of thinking leaves out of its account the rare but fascinating moments in life when exposure to a series of ideas sets a student off on what may turn out to be a lifelong pursuit of a particular set of fantasies and facts—"the defining moment that changed my life". The discussion above also suggests that berating students for being idle and undisciplined may on occasion be correct; at other times however, it may be very wide of the mark. Minds are not solely driven by brains and bodies in the sense of discrete phenomena; they are also driven by conflict and to varying degrees by our ability to resolve such conflicts.

An obvious question comes to mind—wouldn't human beings be better off simply being always rational, reasonable and organised? Shouldn't we insist on the correctness of Copernicus and thus keep trying to keep students in line, "on task" and so forth? This position all too easily turns into the thesis of accountability and quality assurance criticized by Onora O'Neill; as her Reith lectures point out, we may think we are better organised, more efficient and safer. However, the important quality of trusting others to use their fantasies for the benefit of others has been squeezed out of our interactions, leaving us all feeling obscurely lessened and even demoralised by the experience. Whilst order and accountability may be superficially desirable, the aspect of human experience that leads us towards fantasying, imagination, creativity, culture or simply delight in the many wonders of the world are all lost under this regime. Human beings often strive in several directions at the same time and the result of this conflict may be anxiety combined with fantasy or fear linked with creativity. Mind, body and brain often work together but, just as often, they part company with far from predictable results. Allowing fantasy a space in life makes our existence meaningful—meaning arrives with fantasy.

Placebo effects

Although anxiety is superficially less problematic than fantasy in terms of finding appropriately rigorous scientific arguments backed by empirical evidence, a more detailed consideration of the effects of anxiety may lead us to suppose that, if anything, it is actually just as difficult to define and assess. The reason is this: many experiments involving human beings are influenced by a phenomenon known as the "placebo effect". The placebo effect results when the body is "fooled" into healing itself or relieving pain through the combined actions of mind and brain. It is therefore something that offers the opportunity of a feeling of pleasure. A well-known use of the placebo effect is in experiments where it is used as a control to determine whether a drug has better effects in reducing pain than a tablet that looks identical but contains no active ingredients—a placebo. Both groups may report pain relief as a result taking the tablet. Thus, the placebo has a measurable effect that is unconnected with the active ingredients of the tablet. When patients take tablets of any kind, they *expect* the tablet "to do them good".

Placebo effects can of course be measured and adjustments can be made in research to take this effect into account. However, the *causes* of the placebo effect are difficult to separate since many factors may be involved. For example, relief at being offered a tablet is only one of many possible reasons for the reduction of anxiety. Another may be the opportunity to take part in a trial in the first place. Some participants may even feel increased anxiety as a result of being requested to take part in an activity where they know something is being tested but are not sure precisely what that something is. Yet others may feel a general sense of relief that someone is trying to help them at last. In order to avoid unpredictable reactions to experiments caused by both fantasy and anxiety, psychologists often use the tactic of informing participants that their research is aimed at answering one set of questions, when the true aim is something quite different. However, of course, many people are wise to these tactics in these days of instant availability of knowledge from the Internet.

The placebo effect works in a rather similar way to the phenomenon that causes students to delay completing essay assignments. Psychologists refer to it as a "displacement activity". One set of thoughts or fantasies that cause less anxiety, albeit perhaps temporarily, is substituted for a different group of more pressing fears. This interaction of fantasy and anxiety is found in different forms in all areas of human life. Thus, economists ascribe irrational movements of the stock market to "sentiment". This is actually an interestingly vague term that sits uneasily in a discipline much attracted by the lure of supposedly accurate forecasting of the movement of wealth. In this context, "sentiment" describes the unpredictable reaction of large numbers of human beings to events with their normal range of fears about the future as a result of rises in, say, oil prices, the economic effect of war or the illusory "feel-good" factor of the dot.com boom. Nothing will eliminate human reactions such as these. Both fantasies and anxieties are endemic to all experiences in human life.

However, we have not yet finished with placebos. As is well known, the ideas encouraged by the taking of placebos can produce real, measurable physical effects. Many psychologists and neurologists might like to reduce the activities of the mind to bodies controlled by brains, where brains carry out programming. The attribution of problems in life to either nature or nurture is interesting, but, except in a few clear-cut cases such as children born with chromosomal abnormalities, mostly nature interacts with nurture in a fashion that is so intricate that the one influence cannot clearly be separated from the other. This is not a new observation. The father of psychosomatics was Georg Groddeck, a German physician who ran a sanatorium in Baden Baden where he treated patients who suffered from diseases that were indisputably organic in origin such as tuberculosis and syphilis. Groddeck observed that patients suffering from the same disease might experience widely varying symptoms. He argued that this difference was caused by the contribution made by nurture—the environmental background of the individual. Such differences resulted in widely varying symptomatology in the same disease. Groddeck termed this difference "*Das Es*", the "It" in English. The "It" was taken up by Freud and used in his second topography to account for the unconscious something that played an important role in the dispositions of both the conscious and unconscious mind. Strachey rendered *"Das Es"* as "The Id" in English. Here is Groddeck describing "the It" in its various manifestations:

> That the frontiers of science and mysticism get blurred for me in the process, as do the frontiers of body and mind (which for the Greeks, in their heyday, did not exist, by the way), I do not consider a disaster, certainly not for me, because it interests me, and not for my patients, for I help them as far as I am able to, like other doctors . . . And with regard to this I work on the hypothesis that the It makes people ill, because it is pursuing some purpose which it finds useful. When a person has bad breath, his unconscious does not want to be kissed, and when he coughs, it wants something not to happen, and when he vomits, it wants to get rid of something harmful, and when there is a corn, I invariably find a painful spot underneath the corn which the unconscious wants to protect by horny skin. (Groddeck, 1917, p. 40)

This passage may amuse us with its very literal rendering of the equivalence between symptom and thought proposed by Groddeck. Freud proposes the triangulation of the terms used so that the "Id" is not directly represented in the unconscious as anxiety, but only via its unconscious connections with the products of the ego. These in turned are symbolised and capable of entering consciousness through bodily symptoms. It is clear that the "Id", whether Freudian or Groddeckian, is too vague a concept for such research.

However, despite the problems it poses for empirical research, psychosomatics, *inter alia* in the form of the placebo effect is now a flourishing discipline. The placebo effect is an important staging post in the debate about whether psychoanalytic ideas are susceptible to empirical research. A psychoanalytic approach to this argument is that psychoanalysts investigate the nature and construction both of our anxieties *qua* emotional experiences and also analyse the placebos we employ in the form of the fantasies we generate. Psychoanalysis gives us the opportunity to consider experiences in life that are unquantifiable but, nevertheless, very real. Paul Verhaeghe points to some limitations of empirical research into anxiety:

Globally speaking, we can distinguish two major approaches emerging out of Darwin and Freud. From a Darwinian perspective, anxiety is regarded as an inherited, adaptive biological reaction to an external danger. The subsequent development of this idea took place in biomedical research, whose central hypothesis is that every organism displays a homeostatic internal regulation in which anxiety fulfils a survival role. The anxiety-blocking effect of imipramine (D. Klein, 1964, 1980) set the tone for pharmacological research and the accompanying idea of pharmacological treatment. While its therapeutic effects are unmistakable, this line of thought has had a disastrous effect on the clinical psychological study of the phenomenon.

Alongside this we find the Freudian approach, in which anxiety is understood as a reaction to an external and an internal danger, with a focus on the internal (Freud, 1926d). The child's biological helplessness in relation to its own drive impulses that endanger survival is the foundation of anxiety, and this obliges the human being to turn to a number of coping strategies. Any potential psychopathology has to do with these coping strategies, not with the phenomenon of anxiety *per se*. This line of reasoning formed the basis for a number of clinical psychological theories, easily recognized for instance in the contemporary cognitive approach of Beck and Clark [Glas, 2001, p. 24] (Verhaeghe, 2004, p. 260)

Meaning is a close relative of belief. In the chapter on religion, we described the use of belief as a defence against feelings of unsafety. Unsafety arrives when we sense that something or, even worse, everything about our lives might be devoid of meaning; uncertainty has crept in. Most of us find this impossible to contemplate for long periods of time and resort to a belief of some kind, whether religious or not, that imports meaning into our lives. Such belief systems are not necessarily effective in prolonging life, as Gibbon's famous description of the early Christians' resort to suicide as the quickest route to a life hereafter demonstrates. This development was the cue for the early church to make suicide a mortal sin. Alternatively, the activities of today's suicide bombers are all too effective. The cost to themselves and other human beings of extreme religious "certainty" is unspeakably terrible. Equally, however, people often find a world stripped of beliefs meaningless. Belief in something tends toward the creation of meaning and tends therefore towards action of some kind whether physical or mental.

Having a belief in "meaningfulness" may have evolutionary origins. Once human beings arrived at a state of self-consciousness, it would not be evolutionarily helpful to spend our lives simply contemplating our navels—both action and imagination are essential to escape from an overdose of both "real" and existential anxiety. We need to devise ways of escaping death for as long as possible in circumstances where human infants take years to reach sexual maturity and become capable of reproduction.

Conversely, psychology and medicine often attempt to eliminate the influence of the experiential from their explanations of the human world and appeal to certainty by measuring outcomes and difference, ignoring the experiential aspect of many conditions. Indeed, once the word "brain" enters the picture then the idea of measurement comes into play. Perhaps one of the key roles of measurement is to separate ideas of what we normally think of as "brain" activity from "mind" activity, in other words we separate and measure our anxieties to distinguish them from fantasies. Measurement leads us back to the realms of the theory discussed earlier that judgement (measurement of difference) underpins language. What happens when you ask: how can you measure a fantasy? If a fantasy cannot be measured, then what else of value can be said about it? And what happens when you ask: how can you measure anxiety? It is striking that in the latter case, countless facts and figures, research projects and empirical studies are at the disposal of anyone from the informed researcher to the casual internet surfer.

Yet, if we are intelligent brains, why do we spend so much time on activities that are difficult to measure such as daydreaming, fantasising, playing sport, dancing, drinking, watching TV, listening to music and so on? Does "wasting time" in this way actually have an evolutionary gain? A popular answer is of course that play, in the widest sense of the word, is really a means of learning and continuing to learn. However, this answer simply serves to produce two more questions: why should human beings learn to become much more complex thinkers than the rest of the ape family and why should fantasy in the guise of imagination, prediction, forward planning and so forth be developed? What was wrong with being an ape? Nothing—but the capacity to imagine a scenario differently, to predict what will happen tomorrow as a result of today's actions and the development of language as a tool of key importance in these transactions has traced out a new and in evolutionary terms still relatively experimental course for human beings—a course that leads to the creation of meaning in a very different sense from the perceptions of most other animals.

Why does meaning matter?

At the beginning of this book, I made the following statement, "At least one person in six in countries such as Britain or the United States will be diagnosed with a mental illness at some time in their lives; some studies suggest figures as high as one in four. These figures include people suffering the crippling experiences of depression, anorexia, phobia, panic attacks and the like". The vast majority of studies of anxiety take a very literal view of its causes and concentrate on extreme cases typified by post-traumatic stress disorder.

A more detailed account of the prevalence of anxiety, more usually referred to in textbooks in the guise of depression, phobia, panic attacks, PTSD, mental distress and so on can be found on the MIND website which states:

> Estimates of the prevalence of mental distress in Britain vary. The Office for National Statistics or ONS . . . puts the figure at 1 in 6 adults at any one time. Another major survey that is frequently quoted puts the figure at 1 in 4. The 1 in 6 figure given by the ONS represents those people defined as having "significant" mental health problems, whilst the latter survey uses a wider definition of mental health problems. (Goldberg & Huxley, 1992)
>
> In the United States more than 54 million Americans have a mental disorder in any given year although fewer than 8 million seek treatment. (National Mental Health Association, 1999)

Thus, we are very far from regarding anxiety in all its manifestations as "just one of those things". On this account, its effects are serious enough for vast numbers of people to consider anxiety a serious cause for concern in their lives. Clearly, anxiety is not normally considered to be in the same category of thinking as "it's only a day-dream, just a fantasy". The quality of our lives is at stake here, whether measured empirically or subjectively.

The process of opening up and exploring these small, nagging and sometimes irritating distinctions and doubts left behind by much psychological research of an empirical variety constitutes the field of continental philosophy as well as psychoanalysis. There has been much cross-fertilisation between the two disciplines. Philosophy has made use of psychoanalytic insights, particularly those of Freud and Lacan; it acknowledges the validity at least of such questions as the role of the unconscious in the lives of ordinary human beings. Both continental philosophers and psychoanalysts often deride empirical research, since the difficulties of trying to capture the essence or even a whiff of that which escapes easy classification carries its own allure.

As I have indicated earlier, the world of empirical science lists dozens of different mental conditions in psychiatric classification manuals such as DSMIV-TR or its international equivalent ICD-10. Such listings have their place, if only to draw our attention to the huge impact of anxiety on our lives. The differences between many of these classifications are often small and tend to be the focus of discussion at the expense of the wider picture. As a result, users of the manual are encouraged to treat illness as a series of permutations and combinations of apparently objective and discrete phenomena. Such manuals do not and cannot address the issue of how the patients actually experience their worlds as individuals or why each person has a unique and often idiosyncratic way of perceiving the world. This approach unwittingly encourages two developments. Firstly, it becomes expedient to adopt a conservative view of what is normal and acceptable behaviour; certainty about what is normal diminishes our anxiety about "differences"—real or imagined. It is tempting to conflate deviations from the norms laid down by implication in the manual with notions of deviance—not at all the same thing as demonstrated in chapter two where the psychic structure of perversion was discussed. Secondly, this approach leads to an emphasis on the genetic origins of large swathes of mental life at the expense of the effects of the environment. The presence of genetic material can be measured and therefore conveniently objecti-fied; whereas the complex interaction of conscious and unconscious fantasies and anxieties are much more elusive. The nature/nurture debate is insoluble, since from birth and even in the womb, individuals experience widely varying conditions that contribute at least in part to their current experience of life, whereas at least at this point in time, our genetic inheritance is a given. We can do little about "the given"—drugs may alter it somewhat. However, in the vast majority of cases the environment around us constantly alters our perceptions. All talking therapies rely on the often elusive effects of words and transient ideas to change our perceptions of ourselves. Thus, a subjective account of our own state of mind can alter by talking about it to someone else.

Psychoanalysts are therefore interested in the *subjective origins* of what may be *objective differences* in behaviour. To put the same argument very differently, psychoanalysts are interested in how their patients deal with both conscious and unconscious ideas swirling around in their heads and how they relate to the outside world as a consequence. Inside and outside, mind and brain, subjective and objective are often perceived as opposites. However, human beings operate in both states at one and the same time. Anxiety and fantasy combine to express our reactions to this ambiguous state of affairs.

Both psychoanalysis and empirical research often struggle to give an account of the same phenomena from, respectively, subjective and objective positions. In the case of trauma, those who talk about the effects of Post-traumatic Stress Disorder (PTSD) are discussing much the same thing as psychoanalysts who argue about the precise nature of *Nachträglichkeit*. The terminology and the arguments are different but the experience of the sufferer is the same.

To conclude, the search for meaning in anxiety and fantasy always leads to an inescapable conclusion that there is something else. Perhaps we should simply agree with Goethe that "the meaning of life is life".

CHAPTER EIGHT

Fantasy terminable and interminable

Letty is a woman dedicated to her career, that of being a full-time patient. She arrives in her new analyst Laura's consulting room for the first time and says in a subdued but fervent tone, "I hope this will be my last analysis." She recounts a history of frequent hospital visits, suicide attempts, cutting and regular appointments with other psychotherapists, healers and religious gurus. Consequently, she has little time left for love, work or life in general. Letty gives orders to all the members of the helping professions who populate her life—she discharges herself from hospital; she demands that people change their schedules to see her. In her first session, Letty stipulates that Laura see her at least three times a week. She has just arrived in a taxi driven by her boyfriend, Len.

This brief vignette is indicative of the attitude of many patients when they first come to see an analyst. They have a desperate clearly expressed hope that "somebody out there" will "fix" their lives for them. Their expectations, whether direct or implied, are of clear solutions to clear problems that have clear endings.

Thus, "I hope this will be my last analysis" can be understood as a straightforward order to the analyst. It may suggest, "Sort my life out now in double-quick time or I'll kill myself." In parenthesis, Laura will be made to feel that it was all her fault if she allows Letty to die. It could also mean, "I'm not sure I trust you to bring this analysis to an end." This sentiment in turn can be construed either, as "I'm not at all sure I trust anyone" or, as "I'm not sure that I really want my analysis to end at all." Indeed this short sentence is a Freudian "mnemic trace"; a faint "Man Friday" footmark in the sand registering the existence, but not necessarily the presence in consciousness, of many other meanings. At the chronological ending of the analysis, both Letty and Laura will have many more ideas about the possible implications of this phrase. By then, together they will have tracked down some of the hidden unconscious determinants and rendered them available for conscious consideration.

The English phrase "in the last analysis" resonates with meanings. Previous analyses may have been considered, reconsidered, "worked through", accepted, rejected or amended. These are all possibilities. Similarly, the phrase "after all" suggests that, when we have pondered a problem from every angle we can think of, there may be benefits resulting simply from having spent time thinking. Not all final solutions are so comforting. The results of the fascist "final solution" in Nazi Germany were so horrifying that the world is still trying to come to terms with the after-effects. Whether or not we arrive at a definitive answer often depends upon the perspective of the person answering the question. In 1972, the Chinese premier Chou En-Lai was asked what he considered the effects of the French revolution to be on western civilization; he simply observed that it was too early to tell.

On the surface of things, the end of an anxiety, the end of a fantasy and the end of an analysis are simple and clear phenomena. The footprint in the sand may disappear with the oncoming tide. Its existence ends. However, the implications of the footprint linger. Robinson Crusoe is now alerted to the fact that he is not always alone on his island and his thinking and behaviour are both permanently altered as result. These considerations inform Freud's paper, "Analysis Terminable and Interminable". As with many of Freud's complex ideas, the very possibility of a clear conclusion (in both senses of the term) is a well-nigh impossible position to reach. He puts forward the following proposition:

> We must first of all decide what is meant by the ambiguous phrase "the end of an analysis". From a practical standpoint it is easy

to answer. An analysis is ended when the analyst and the patient cease to meet each other for the analytic session. This happens when two conditions have been approximately fulfilled: first that the patient shall no longer be suffering from his symptoms and shall have overcome his anxieties and his inhibitions; and secondly, that the analyst shall judge that so much repressed material has been made conscious, so much that was unintelligible has been explained, and so much internal resistance conquered, that there is no need to fear a repetition of the pathological processes concerned. If one is prevented by external difficulties from reaching this goal, it is better to speak of an *incomplete* analysis rather than of an *unfinished* one. (Freud, 1937c, p. 219, italics in the original)

A striking feature of this quotation is that Freud is speaking about questions of approximation and degree. There is no indication that the patient will be cured in the sense that when a person recovers from a cold they no longer have any symptoms. If an analysis brings about a *relative* change, how then can a conclusion be reached about an *absolute* ending except in literal physical terms? The mind's conflicts tend to linger on.

In the pages preceding this quotation, Freud discusses the fate of his famous patient, the Wolf Man, whose first analysis ended, principally, because Freud set a date for its termination. This analysis did not prevent the recurrence of some of the patient's distressing symptoms. As a result of the Russian Revolution of 1917 the Wolf Man lost his vast estates in Russia and became penniless. The "incoming tide" of the earlier analysis had washed away his most troubling ideas but the existence in the unconscious of hidden forces made themselves felt when times changed. The savages returned to Robinson Crusoe's island and the "internal savages" in the Wolf Man's mind reappeared. Freud himself seems rather ambivalent about the effect of his first analysis of the Wolf Man. He reports:

When, towards the end of the war, he returned to Vienna, a refugee and destitute, I had to help him to master a part of the transference which had not been resolved. This was accomplished in a few months, and . . . "since then the patient has felt normal and has behaved unexceptionably, in spite of the war having robbed him of his home, his possessions, and all his family relationships". (Freud, 1937c, p. 218)

And yet, he continues,

But several times during this period his good state of health has been interrupted by attacks of illness which could only be construed as offshoots of his perennial neurosis. Thanks to the skill of one of my pupils, Dr. Ruth Mack Brunswick, a short course of treatment has on each occasion brought these conditions to an end. (Freud, 1937c, p. 218)

Freud links the effectiveness of analysis to questions of a person's innate constitution (about which very little can currently can be done) and the nature and degree of a patient's previous traumatic experiences. He refers to "altering" and "taming" the ego (Freud, 1937c, p. 220) through analytic intervention. In other words, only the influences derived from subsequent internal conflicts, no doubt affected by external environmental factors (such as losing one's fortune as the result of a revolution) can be addressed.

There is a subtle point embedded in Freud's discussion hinted at by his English translator, Strachey. In a footnote, Strachey comments that the original German is *Nachverdrängung* (after-repression) whereas in the "Repression" paper and elsewhere the term used is *Nachdrängen* (after-pressure) (Freud, 1937c, p. 227). A careful dissection of these terms suggests that the first, *Nachverdrängung*, refers to the symptoms that are left behind, the footmarks in the sand, that tell the tale of what went before. The second suggests that a continuous pressure remains that is continuously experienced by the patient—as if Robinson Crusoe could not excise the image of the footprint from his mind and it continued to haunt him. The first is an example of something that is a given—the footprint exists, regardless of Crusoe observing it. The second is an effect leaving a last impression in Crusoe's mind. Characteristically, Freud is arguing for both positions—as the mood takes him, leaving the reader free to accept or reject either theory. Perhaps in the clinic we aim to offer the patient the possibility of a choice of perceptions about her unique experience of living. The choice, in ideal circumstances, is then a decision to be made by the patient herself, not the analyst.

In the same paper, Freud recounts the story of a woman who was cured of a hysterical inability to walk. Later surgery for a gynae-cological condition prompted a return to a hysterical neurosis. Freud says of this episode, "I am inclined to think that, were it not for the new trauma, there would have been no fresh outbreak of neurosis" (Freud, 1937c, pp. 222–3). According to Freud therefore, a new trauma can reactivate an old symptom when both analyst and analysand may have concluded that the analysis had ended success-fully. The memory of the footprint in the sand no doubt returned all too vividly to Crusoe when he sees the savages. Does this mean that the work of "altering" and "taming" the ego was insufficient or ineffective? Should this woman's analysis really have continued? It is interesting to note a few pages later that Freud observes:

All repressions take place in childhood . . . In later years no fresh repressions are carried out; but the old ones persist, and their services continue to be made use of by the ego for mastering the instincts. New conflicts are disposed of by what we call "after-repression". (Freud, 1937c, p. 227)

The conclusion may be drawn that, whilst trauma can revisit us in new forms and thereby drastically change our perception of our-selves and of the world around us, our basic methods of repression never change. In his paper, "Repression", (Freud, 1915d) this argument is developed more fully. Freud makes a distinction here between "primal repression" (which presumably takes place at the earliest stages of life) and a second stage of repression, "repression proper". It would appear from Freud's account that changes to "repression proper" could conceivably take place during analysis whilst "primal repression" is subject to "fixation" and consequently, cannot be directly addressed (Freud, 1915d, p. 148). Freud does not really take up this issue—rather he gives examples of anxiety hysteria, conversion hysteria and obsessional neurosis. Are these conditions examples of secondary rather than primary repression, or secondary repression in tandem with primary repression? In each, repression operates differently with respect to the prevention or diminution of anxiety, giving rise to distinctive symptomatology in each case.

If Freud considers that trauma can revisit a patient and dramatic-ally change their life regardless of a previous analysis, why should he not concede that a change in the capacity for repression (whether represented by an increase or a decrease) would not have a similarly noticeable effect? Indeed, he seems to admit precisely this point in his later paper, "Analysis Terminable and Interminable" (Freud, 1937c, p. 227). This throws into question then, the distinction between "primal repression" and "repression proper". If the nature of the patient's repression *can* be changed, then at what point can a distinction be made between a primal repression and subsequent repressions?

It may appear at first that this argument is leading us away from the thorny problem of the end, or otherwise, of analysis. However, if repression is on a continuum, then the argument for the end of analysis as being anything other than an arbitrary decision becomes an issue of central importance.

The question of whether Freud's stress on primacy is correct or not has implications for the ending of analysis from yet another perspective. Returning to the dialectical theme, Freud argues that the dialectical process starts with the cries of the infant. The cry sets in chain a whole series of events, some of them with temporary consequences and others that have a permanent effect on the well-being of the individual. A dialectical process could be envisaged as a branching effect, each thesis and antithesis leading to a choice that in turn produces another thesis and antithesis. Freud's philosophical position is that of an essentialist. He believes that there is an originating moment to these dialectical processes, whether it is a matter of repression (primary repression), narcissism (primary narcissism) or the primal scene (primary "trauma"). T. S. Eliot's poem, "East Coker", the second of *Four Quartets* starts with the sentence "In my beginning is my end". It closes with, "In my end is my beginning". Either the dialectical process is endless and in some possibly spiritual sense, circular: or they begin somewhere; and if they have a specific beginning, is this beginning, in itself of significance?

A similar wavering with regard to another key term in Freud's lexicon, namely, "the strengthening of the ego" is also noticeable in "Analysis Terminable and Interminable". Freud introduces this phrase early in the paper, "Only when a case is a predominantly traumatic one will analysis succeed in doing what it is so superlatively able to do ... thanks to having strengthened the patient's ego" (Freud, 1937c, p. 220). However, fifteen pages later he admits:

> The ego, if we are to be able to make such a pact [for treatment] with it, must be a normal one. But a normal ego of this sort is, like normality in general, an ideal fiction. The abnormal ego, which is unserviceable for our purposes, is unfortunately no fiction. Every normal person, in fact, is only normal on the average. (Freud, 1937c, p. 235)

If a normal ego is a fiction, then what is it that analysis might strengthen? A reasonable reading of this argument might lead one to think that strengthening an abnormal ego could conceivably even be a damaging process.

Freud describes repression as a process that holds sway between the pleasure and unpleasure impulses. Similarly he depicts the ego as "ceasing to support our efforts at uncovering the id; it opposes them, disobeys the fundamental rule of analysis, and allows no further derivatives of the repressed to emerge" (Freud, 1937c, p. 239). The ego is therefore at best an unreliable and temporary ally in analysis.

Since the exploration of the concept of repression and of the ego have both yielded ambiguous results in pursuit of a rationale for ending analysis, Freud changes tack and introduces the death drive (instinct)[1] into the discussion:

> It is not a question of an antithesis between an optimistic and a pessimistic theory of life. Only by the concurrent or mutually opposing action of the two primal instincts—Eros and the death-instinct—, never by one or the other alone, can we explain the rich multiplicity of the phenomena of life. (Freud, 1937c, p. 243)

Again Freud resorts to stating an argument in terms of two extreme opposing theories and then tempering the debate with the intro-

---

1 Most readers who are familiar with the Strachey translation will know that a more precise if still not completely acceptable translation of the German "Trieb" is "drive" rather than "instinct".

duction of relative positions whose connection back to the original theories is always left unclear. Thus referring us back to the "cosmic phantasy" of Empedocles does not solve the problem of whether agglomeration or fusion take place in the unconscious—Freud uses both terms to describe the effects of Empedocles' thought (Freud, 1937c, p. 246). Either way, in order to promote the idea of a clear path to(wards) the end of analysis, Freud tries to place markers like "primal repression", "the strengthening of the ego" and the "death drive" so that the reader is lighted on his way in the direction of a clear and definite conclusion. Each of these terms fails as a marker, since each is founded upon an imprecision. Regretfully, therefore, we must conclude that Freud's heroic effort to institute a logical ending to analysis fails.

As in so many other instances, Freud introduced an important theoretical concept into psychoanalysis and then Lacan took up the original idea and turned it into something rather different and sometimes only tangentially connected to Freud's original formulation. The problematic of the ending of analysis interested Lacan just as much as Freud. Since Lacan's later definitions of what constitutes analysis depart radically from that of Freud, an ending is the conclusion of some quite different experience. A Lacanian psychoanalyst, Anne Dunand, suggests that the timing of Lacan's *Seminar XI, The Four Fundamental Concepts of Psychoanalysis*, is vitally important to the development of his thinking on this topic since this seminar marks the point when he parted company with the International Psychoanalytical Association (IPA) (Dunand, 1995, p. 244). By the 1960s, Lacan's view of psychoanalysis was already on a course that would lead to a radical redefinition of its aims and purposes and consequently his split from the IPA. The IPA had formed a view that it was desirable to encourage the patient to fall in love with the analyst, in order that the early neuroses connected with their love relationships would be repeated in the analysis. It would then be the analyst's task to make interpretations, which would gradually expose this "falling in love" as a chimera. From the first, Lacan doubted the wisdom of actively encouraging "new love" in the analysand. Indeed, he considered that, wherever possible, the identification of the patient with the analyst—"falling in love with the analyst"—should gradually be dismantled. Rather than focussing on the transference love directed at the analyst, Lacan centred his work around (re)searching the underlying structure of the symptomatology of the analysand. The task of analysis then becomes the work of analysing this structure in order to uncover the misconceptions of the analysand that have led to the formation of the structure. However, the structure itself (the fundamental fantasy in Lacanian terminology) will never go away. Anne Dunand sets out Lacan's position clearly:

> If there is such a thing as the end of treatment, if analysis is not interminable, if a point can be reached where it can be described as an irreversible process, then its structure has to be defined, and what is expected has to be outlined and specified. (Dunand, 1995, p. 243)

If we agree with this statement, then we have to turn to those pages in Lacan where he carries out this project. If the content of analysis is radically altered then, by the same token, the means of bringing it to an end and the accompanying theory of the termination of analysis will also change.

In Lacan's view the end of analysis involves "traversing the fundamental fantasy". A fundamental fantasy is a curious phrase since it refers to an 'underlying structure that has no specific content in itself' (Verhaeghe, 2004, p. 373). The concepts of "inside" and "outside", "internal" and "external" are shown to be highly problematic in Lacan's hands; he uses the phenomenon of the Möbius strip to illustrate the movement of the psyche from one "face" to the other. A Möbius strip is a narrow strip of paper where the two ends of the strip are joined together so that it has a 180 degree twist. It is now possible to start at a point A on the surface and trace out a path with your finger that passes through the point which is apparently on the other side of the surface from A. Contrary to intuitive expectation however, there is only one surface. Moreover, this surface has no "beginning" and no "end". It is still worth keeping in mind that two surfaces are what we think we see and expect. Thus, Lacan shows that fantasy is internal and external at the same time and travels seamlessly between the two (fantasised) surfaces or registers. The second purpose of traversing the fundamental fantasy is to allow the patient gradually to reduce the "slippage" between what he wishes for in life (desire) and what he actually finds himself doing (drive). A patient progresses beyond the apparent impasse of the symptoms produced by the disjunction between drive and desire, by gradually discovering that his or her desire can be more attuned to drive.

Lacan invented the concept of "the Pass" in contradistinction to Freud's notion that analysis was in some senses interminable. "The Pass" can only be negotiated via the traversal of the fundamental fantasy. It is interesting to note that there does not seem to be one single text in Lacan that sets out a coherent theory. *Seminar XIV La Logique du Fantasme 1966–1967*, discusses the role of the Möbius strip but not the Pass as such. "The Pass" was conceptualised at the same time as his Seminar, "Proposition du 9 Octobre 1967 sur le psycho-analyste de l'École", Scilicet, No. 1 (1968) pp. 14–30. "The Pass" is a tool whereby a person justifies his right to practice as an analyst. It is *not* a concept that is directly connected to the question of traversal of the fundamental fantasy. Whilst a Lacanian analysis clearly leads to a very different formulation from Freud's, there still seems to be an unresolved problem with regard to ending the process. Does one conclude that the only end to a Lacanian analysis is to negotiate the Möbius strip? Yet, the point of the analogy is surely to demonstrate the lack of fixed points in the human psyche. Furthermore, how would one define such a journey since much of what "happens" in analysis remains unconscious and incomplete?

Gradually, the conclusion that the end of analysis—however defined—is simply arbitrary, becomes more compelling. In this instance, both Freud and Lacan leave something to be desired—rather it is Ferenczi, with his customary style and charm, who offers a refreshingly different perspective:

While dealing with a patient who, apart from certain neurotic difficulties, came to analysis chiefly because of certain abnormalities and peculiarities of his character, I suddenly discovered, incidentally after more than eight months, that he had been deceiving me the whole time in connexion with an important circumstance of a financial nature. At first this caused me the greatest embarrassment. The fundamental rule of analysis, on which the whole of our technique is built up, calls for the true and complete communication by the patient of all his ideas and associations. What, then, is one to do if the patient's pathological condition consists precisely in mendacity? (Ferenczi, 1955, p. 77)

Ferenczi goes on to recount that when he taxes his patient with his lying, the patient cannot remember the relevant events relating to the lies. Ferenczi concludes that the patient has split off the material containing the lies since they are too painful to bring into consciousness.

There is a fascinating footnote at this point in the text. Ferenczi posits the idea that compulsive liars, "have several super-egos which have failed to fuse. Even scholars who do not *a priori* deny the possibility of 'many truths' about the same thing are probably people whose scientific morality has not developed into a unity" (Ferenczi, 1955, p. 78). Thus, he raises the idea that distinguishing between truth and falsehood is even more problematic than we might already think. Incidentally, this view chimes well with the multiple belief systems that operate in New Age believers discussed in the chapter on religious belief.

Ferenczi's argument continues to proceed in direction of an examination of the distinction between lying and truth. He starts with the infant, "What in the light of morality and of the reality principle we call a lie, in the case of an infant and in terms of pathology we call a fantasy" (Ferenczi, 1955, p. 79). If the classical treatment of hysteria lies in uncovering the false connections that lead back into infancy, then when we look forwards, the way in which the patient unconsciously structures *everything* about their world in terms of a lie comes as no surprise.

If the patient can arrive at the perception that everything that he has thought to be axiomatically true about his life is incorrect, then he has reached a point at which he/she no longer needs analysis. Thus for Ferenczi, the end of analysis comes at the point when a patient gives up the pleasure of unconsciously believing in a fictional account of their life. Unlike the theories of Freud and Lacan, Ferenczi's view offers a possibility of a reasoned solution to the problem of the end of analysis.

A provisional hypothesis embracing Ferenczi's ideas might envisage the end of analysis as incorporating the following. Firstly, a particular kind of fantasising where the patient's search for "truth" is less embroiled in the conflicting demands of his or her superego and id. Secondly, the patient can acknowledge that what is true for him may not be true for others. Finally there may be a realisation that the truths that are arrived at are partial and have lingering and enduring effects on both the subject and the other. All these arguments presuppose that the fantasies that cause us most pain are susceptible to interpretation and that thereby they can be altered.

In the cases of psychosis and perversion the end of the analysis must be very different. As indicated in chapter two, these fantasies are of a different order and are not susceptible to change through interpretations along conventional neurotic lines. The dialectical approach implicit in such thinking will not work because the relationship of truth to falsehood is not dialectical in these cases. It is arguable, that in both perversion and psychosis there can be no end to an analysis since neither structure allows a dialectical engagement with the analyst to be introduced in the first place.

We do not live in an ideal world where those who suffer (most of us) can spend unlimited amounts of time and money on psychoanalysis. Most of us have multiple belief systems; working out the complicated way in which such beliefs interact with each other can sometimes take years. Publicly funded psychotherapy is often very helpful but it is usually limited in duration and operates mainly in situations where people need emergency help. As a result, some patients live lives that are quite patently a completely false account of their real experience or feel completely crippled by phobia or compulsive thoughts. However, it is a bold and foolish analyst— although there are some of these around—who tampers with the fantasies of these people without great care and trepidation. Some people exhibit great emotional suffering but their suffering may be increased rather than relieved if they are brought face to face with the truth of their fantasies. Fantasy frequently serves as a protection against unbearable anxiety. Short-term time-limited psychotherapy with or without a drug regime may be better than nothing, but nevertheless this can lead to the "revolving door" syndrome where patient becomes just well enough to finish a course of therapy only to relapse and come back for more treatment.

Like Lacan, Ferenczi has observations to make about analysts in training in relation to the end of analysis. According to Ferenczi, the patient will perceive that the analyst is consistent and truthful in his dealing with the transference and the patient. As a result of "a fully completed analysis", "the analyst . . . must know and be in control of even the most recondite weaknesses of his own character" (Ferenczi 1955, p. 84). However, the analyst is also a human being and therefore susceptible to the fact that we all live in a world made sense of through our own individualised and, to some degree, fantastical constructions. How can any of us ever arrive at the end of our private non-stop showing in our heads of the world rearranged to our liking?

There is a further problem with the end of the analysis. Who is ending it and what is being brought to an end? It is sometimes the case that private practice can be an opportunity to practice interminable analysis. Cut and dried endings are not an option so patients stay interminably. It is notable that the "long" six month analysis of Freud's time has been replaced by the "long" ten or more years of Kleinian, or Lacanian analysis. Psychotherapists and psychoanalysts often borrow from the world of medical terminology and describe their clients as patients. This description is often more accurate than our patients might wish since they may "patiently" visit the consulting room of their analyst for years in search of a complete analysis, i.e. one that has an "ending". Many people seeking a solution to their pressing emotional problems will ask a therapist or analyst at the beginning, "How long will it be before I will feel better?" The most truthful reply might be "as long as a piece of string". In other words, we cannot tell them. The patient must be patient. This problem exercised Freud from the beginning. In *Studies in Hysteria*, he discovered that simply explaining to a patient the likely causes of her suffering might remove the symptoms temporarily, but after a short while they bounced back as if the patient had never heard what he said in the first place. Over a hundred years of psychoanalysis has produced a slightly more sophisticated understanding of why this should be, but has not altered the problem; namely, in "real" life, nothing can be changed instantly. In the life of our wishes and fantasies, we can play havoc with the rules of times and change things to suit the circumstances we confront in relation to our prejudices and anxieties.

As discussed earlier in the context of the fantasies enacted in Star Trek, many people wish that they could simply make their lives "otherwise" that they lived in any time other than "now". There is the lure of desire, opening up the wish for change—if only I could wake up and find that various unpalatable facts pertaining to my life have been changed for me overnight without any effort on my part. No wonder our patients often wish they could be over and done with analysis in a couple of hours. This fantasy always fails since, despite our wish to stand still, our minds are on the move in a constantly changing world and even the most unimaginative mind ranges over a vast terrain far greater than can be compressed into a couple of weeks.

There are further considerations regarding the phenomenon of waiting. The first is that as the nursery rhyme of *Oranges and lemons* indicates, questions often simply elicit further questions. Many patients hope that analysis will supply answers. However, much of the time it changes the kinds of questions patients ask themselves rather than supplying answers. As Lacan frequently remarks, the patient puts the analyst in the place of the *"sujet supposé savoir"*, the subject who is supposed to know. Yet what is the "it" that the subject is supposed to know? What is the "it" that keeps us in a state of continuously wanting to know what the subject is supposed to know? The experience of waiting, being patient and being a patient all serve to postpone, sometimes indefinitely, the possibility of arriving at knowledge and at solutions.

Patients meeting an analyst for the first time frequently arrive with a series of problems. It is a well-known fact that this initial presentation often turns out to have only a tangential connection with the issues that turn out to be at the heart of her suffering. Equally, it has often been observed that an apparently irrelevant fact perhaps dropped into the conversation with the analyst as an afterthought may turn out to hold the key to the patient's suffering.

Let us return to Letty once more. We examined a few of the possible meanings of her statement that she hoped that this would be "her last analysis". At the end of her analysis she has found time to switch careers. She no longer fends off death by courting it in suicide attempts. She has gained a qualification in a profession allied to medicine and now relieves the physical pain of others rather than inflicting it upon herself. She has ditched her abusive boyfriend who had continued to bully her following her brother Leo's tradition. She has spent many hours in the consulting room painfully working through her brother's abuse of her. The abuse, like the analysis, has ended. The effects of the abuse have probably not disappeared completely. As in the case of the Wolf Man, they may reappear later in Letty's life, probably at a time of difficulty for her.

Life is full of apparent oppositions and contradictions: one aspect of the analyst's task is to expose the fallacious nature of these contradictions. When Letty says, "one part of me thinks that I was bullied but another part of me thinks that I do the bullying", actually *both parts* constitute different aspects or perspectives of the whole. Yet, life is more than the sum of its parts. Lacan's topological approach embodied in the Möbius strip pays dividends here since it enables us to think of the interplay of surfaces, of the meaning of words crossing and re-crossing each other.

Why should the presenting problem be different from the later problems disclosed in an analysis? Why must both patient and analyst wait to find out what these are? And why does the patient imagine that the analyst knows the answers? A moment's reflection tells us that of course the only expert on an individual version of suffering is the person who is the subject of that suffering, so of course the analyst cannot *really* know the answers.

Conclusion

Throughout this book, there is an attempt to keep the three themes of fantasy, anxiety and psychoanalysis either in the forefront of our thinking or at least lurking in the background as one of Freud's "mnemic traces". Our human addiction to distractions of all kinds, especially stories with the ability to transmute our pain, has meant that, if given half a chance, fantasy tends to dominate the proceedings. However, as I hope I have shown, our stories are often a poisoned chalice. We can lift a goblet overflowing with ambrosia to our lips, but hemlock or simply vinegar may be what we find ourselves drinking.

In another mode, we can persuade ourselves that reality is awful, terrifying and inescapable; lest we forget this reality, we endure constant reminders of it by sinking into the depths of depression, cutting ourselves, starving ourselves, or even throwing ourselves into war with martyrdom as our aim. The anxiety may not always be present in consciousness but it is perennially there all the same.

Those of us who pass for sane—so long as the strange and bizarre fantasies we entertain are not displayed too publicly—oscillate between the poles of fantasy and anxiety. Even fantasy as nightmare is a distraction from the Real. Throughout this book, I have favoured the operation of both conscious and unconscious negative dialectics as the principle explanation for this movement in ourselves, and in the world outside. Everything keeps changing and we always keep trying to moderate if not stabilise the inherently unstable experience that is called living. The other mode of thinking that interposes itself from time to time is our wish to pretend that things can fuse together be the same, be just like someone or something else.

However, being just like someone else is never the whole story. Our differences make us different and isolated in an existential sense from everyone else. As is well known, identical twins have many attributes that they share as well as their outward appearance. Interestingly however, their genes do not mean that they choose partners with similar personalities. Difference rather than similarity is the engine of life. In Freudian terms, the first belongs on the side of the life drive and the second aligns itself with the death drive.

Psychoanalysis as both a theory and practice often lurks in the shadows of this book. There are other discourses and other theories that have much to contribute to an understanding of both fantasy and anxiety. Those theories that dismiss it with a contemptuous smirk, "Well, where's the evidence?" often have nothing to say about the stuff of dreams. Much of most people's ordinary experiences such as gossiping at work, talking about the exploits of their favour soap actors (both in their TV characters and in real life), idling speculating about how they may spend their holidays, wondering what the next-door-neighbour's wife might be like in bed and so forth—endlessly—can at least be given a hearing by psychoanalysis. In fact the major experiences of life such as whom to love, a choice of career, the political destiny of countries are also clearly intertwined with fantasy and anxiety. These issues too form the stuff of psychoanalytic discourse. Such facts about our lives, whether trivial or vital, are not necessarily evidence for anything except, as Hamlet said:

There are more things in heaven and earth, Horatio,
Than are dreamt of in your philosophy.

(Hamlet I, v, 166–7)

REFERENCES

American Psychiatric Association, (2000). *Diagnostic and Statistical Manual of Mental Disorders,* fourth edition, Text Revision. Washington, DC: American Psychiatric Association.

Austen, J. (1817). *Northanger Abbey.* Paris: Zulma Classics, 2005.

Bacon, F. (1625). Of Death. In: *Bacon's Essays.* London: Morley's Universal Library, 1889.

Baldick, C. (1992). *The Oxford Book of Gothic Tales.* Oxford: Oxford University Press.

Banks, Iain. (1984). *The Wasp Factory.* London: Macmillan.

Banks, Iain M. (1987). *Consider Phlebas.* London: Macmillan.

Benton, T & Craib, I. (2001). *The Philosophy of Social Science.* Basingstoke: Palgrave.

Breuer, J. and Freud, S. (1895d). *Studies on Hysteria, S.E., 2.*

Budd, S. (1977). *Varieties of Unbelief: Atheists and Agnostics in English Society 1850–1960.* London: Heinemann.

Burgoyne, B. (2000). Autism and Topology. In: B. Burgoyne (Ed.), *Drawing the Soul: Schemas and Models in Psychoanalysis.* London: Rebus Press.

Carter, A. (1979). *The Sadeian Woman: An Exercise in Cultural History.* London: Virago.

Charraud, N. (2000). A Calculus of Convergence. In: B. Burgoyne (Ed.), *Drawing the Soul: Schemas and Models in Psychoanalysis.* London: Rebus Press.

Churchill, C. (1997). *Blue Heart.* London: Nick Hern Books.

Damasio, A.R. (2000). *The Feeling of What Happens.* London: Vintage.

Dawkins, R. (1976). *The Selfish Gene.* Oxford: OUP. New Edn. 1989.

171

Dawkins, R. & Coyne, (2005). J. "One side can be wrong" in *The Guardian* Life Section. September 1st, 2005, p. 5.

Dinnerstein, D. (1976). *The Mermaid and the Minotaur*. New York: Harper Row.

Dunand, A. (1995). The End of Analysis (I). In: (Eds.), R. Feldstein, B. Fink, & M. Jaanus, *Reading Seminar XI: Lacan's Four Fundamental Concepts of Psychoanalysis* (pp. 243–9). NY: SUNY.

Durkheim, E. (1912). *The Elementary Forms of Religious Life*. (Trans.). C. Cosman, Oxford: Oxford University Press, 2001.

Eliot, T.S. (1943) *Four Quartets*, London: Faber & Faber.

Fairbairn, W. R. D. (1952). *Psychoanalytic Studies of the Personality*. London: Routledge.

Ferenczi S. (1927). The Problem of the Termination of the Analysis. In: *Final Contributions to the Problems and Methods of Psycho-Analysis*, (Trans.). J. Dupont, London: Hogarth, 1955.

Fink, B., (1997). *A Clinical Introduction to Lacanian Analysis, Theory and Technique*. Cambridge, Massachusetts: Harvard University Press.

Fonagy, P., Gergely, G., Jurist, E., & Target, M. (2004). *Affect Regulation, Mentalization and the Development of the Self*. London: Karnac.

Forrester, J. (1980). *Language and the Origins of Psychoanalysis*. London: MacMillan.

Freud, S. *The Standard Edition of the Complete Psychological Works of Sigmund Freud* (S.E.). James Strachey (Trans.). London: the Hogarth Press.

Freud, S. (1894a). The Neuro-Psychoses of Defence. *S.E.*, 3.

Freud, S. & Breuer, J., (1895d) *Studies on Hysteria*. S.E., 2.

Freud, S. (1900a). *Interpretation of Dreams*. S.E., 4 -5.

Freud, S. (1901b). *The Psychopathology of Everyday Life*. S.E., 6.

Freud, S. (1905c). *Jokes and Their Relation to the Unconscious*. S.E. 8.

Freud, S. (1910a). Five Lectures on Psychoanalysis. *S.E.*, 11.

Freud, S. (1911c). Psychoanalytic Notes on an Autobiographical Account of a Case of Paranoia (Dementia Paranoides). *S.E.*, 12.

Freud, S. (1914g). Remembering, Repeating and Working-Through. *S.E.*, XII.

Freud, S. (1915d). Repression. *S.E.*, 14.

Freud, S. (1918a). The Taboo of Virginity. *S.E.*, 11.

Freud, S. (1918b). *From the History of an Infantile Neurosis*. S.E. 17.

Freud, S. (1919h). The Uncanny. *S.E.*, 17.

Freud, S. (1920g). *Beyond The Pleasure Principle*. S.E., 18.

Freud, S. (1921c). *Group Psychology and the Analysis of the Ego*. S.E., 18.

Freud, S. (1925h). Negation. *S.E., 19.*

Freud, S. (1926d). *Inhibitions, Symptoms and Anxiety. S.E., 20.*

Freud, S. (1930a). *Civilization and its Discontents. S.E., 21.*

Freud, S. (1937c). Analysis Terminable and Interminable. *S.E., 23.*

Freud, S. (1950a). A Project for a Scientific Psychology. *S.E., 1.*

Freud, S. (2002). *The Schreber Case.* A. Phillips, (Ed.) (Trans.). A. Webber, Introduction MacCabe, C. London: Penguin Classics.

Frost, R. (1920). The Road Not Taken. In: *Mountain Interval* New York: Henry Holt & Co.

Gibbon, E. (2000 [1788]) *The Decline and Fall of the Roman Empire,* London: Penguin Classics.

Glas, G. (2001). *Angst.* Amsterdam: Boom.

Goldberg, D. and Huxley, P. (1992). *Common Mental Disorders: a bio-social model.* London: Routledge.

Harari, R. (2001). *Lacan's Seminar on "Anxiety": An Introduction,* New York: Other Press.

Heidegger, M. (1978). What is Metaphysics? In: D. Farrell Krell, (Ed.), *Basic Writings.* London: Routledge.

Hofstadter, D.R. & Dennett, D.C. (1981). *The Mind's I: Fantasies and Reflections on Self and Soul,* New York: Basic Books.

Humphrey, N. (1992). *A History of Mind.* New York: Copernicus.

Ibsen, H. (1881) *Ghosts,* trans. M. Meyer, London: Methuen, 1991.

Isaacs, S. (1952). The Nature and Function of Phantasy. In: M. Klein, P. Heimann, S. Isaacs , S. & Riviere, J. *Developments in Psychoanalysis* (pp. 67–121). London: Karnac Books, 1989.

Itchy and Scratchy website: www.snpp.com/episodes/9F03.html

James, W. (1902). *The Varieties of Religious Experience: A Study in Human Nature.* London: Penguin, 1982.

Jameson, F. (1977). In: S. Felman, (Ed.), *Literature and Psychoanalysis: The Question of Reading Otherwise.* Baltimore, MD: John Hopkins University Press.

Klein, D.F. (1964). Delineation of two-drug responsive anxiety syndromes. *Psychopharmacologiea* 5: 397–408.

Klein, D.F. (1980). Anxiety reconceptualized. *Comprehensive Psychiatry* 21: 411–27.

Klein, M. (1928). Early Stages of the Oedipus Conflict. In: *Love, Guild and Reparation and Other Works 1921–1945.* London: Hogarth, 1975.

Klein, M. (1930). The Importance of Symbol-Formation in the Development of the Ego. In: *Love, Guild and Reparation and Other Works 1921–1945.* London: Hogarth, 1975.

O.Neill, O. (2002). *A Question of Trust: The BBC Reith Lectures 2002.* Cambridge: Cambridge University Press.

Lacan, J. (1968). *Speech and Language in Psychoanalysis.* (Trans.). A. Wilden, Baltimore: The John Hopkins University Press.

Lacan, J. (1977). *Écrits—A Selection.* (Trans.). A. Sheridan, London: Routledge.

Lacan, J. (1988 [1954–55]). *The Seminar of Jacques Lacan: Book II The Ego in Freud's Theory and in the Technique of Psychoanalysis 1954–1955.* Cambridge: Cambridge University Press.

Lacan, J. (1962–63). *Seminar X "L'Angoisse".* Private translation: C. Gallagher, Unpublished Seminar.

Laplanche, J. & Pontalis, J.-B. (1973). *The Language of Psychoanalysis.* (Trans.). D. Nicholson-Smith. London: Karnac.

Laplanche, J. (1992). *Seduction, Translation and the Drives.* (Eds.) J. Fletcher & M. Stanton. London: Institute of Contemporary Arts.

Laplanche, J. (1999). The Unfinished Copernican Revolution. In: *Essays on Otherness.* (Ed.) & (Trans.). J. Fletcher, London: Routledge.

Lévi-Strauss, C. (1958). *Anthropologie Structurale.* Paris: Librairie Plon.

Lévi-Strauss, C. (1963). *Structural Anthropology.* (Trans.). C. Jacobson & B. Grundfest Schoepf, NY: Basic Books.

Lewis, B. (2002). *What Went Wrong? Western Impact and Middle Eastern Response.* London: Phoenix.

More, T. (1516). *Utopia.* (Trans.). P. Turner, London: Penguin, 1965.

Morris, W. (1891). *News from Nowhere.* London: Penguin Classics. 1998.

National Mental Health Association. (1999). *Factsheet: Mental Illness and the Family.* www.nmha.org/infoctr/factsheets.

Office for National Statistics. (2000). "Psychiatric Morbidity Among Adults Living in Private Households in Great Britain". London: www.mind.org.uk.

Orwell, G. (1949). *Nineteen Eighty-Four.* London: Secker & Warburg.

Panksepp, J. (1998). *Affective Neuroscience: The Foundations of Human and Animal Emotions.* Oxford: Oxford University Press.

Parmenides, (1984) *Parmenides of Elea: Fragments,* (Trans.). D. Gallop, Toronto, University of Toronto Press.

Piontelli, A. (1992). *From Fetus to Child: An Observational and Psychoanalytic Study.* London: Routledge.

Pullman, P. (2000). *The Amber Spyglass.* London: Scholastic Press.

Radcliffe, A. (1794). *The Mysteries of Udolpho.* Introduction, T. Castle, Oxford: Oxford University Press, 1994.

Rowling, J. K. *Harry Potter and the Order of the Phoenix* London: Bloomsbury, 2003.

Solms, M. (2000). Dreaming and REM sleep are controlled by different brain mechanisms. In: *Behavioral and Brain Science.* 23, (6): 843–50.

Stevenson, R. L. (1885). Olalla. In: C. Baldick. *The Oxford Book of Gothic Tales.* Oxford: Oxford University Press, 1992.

Stoker, B. (1897). *Dracula.* Boston, MA: Bedford/St. Martin's, 2002.

Thurber, J. (1945). *The Secret Life of Walter Mitty and Other Pieces.* London: Penguin.

Thurston, L. Sinthome. In: D. Evans, (1996). *An Introductory Dictionary of Lacanian Psychoanalysis.* London: Routledge.

Schreber, D. P. (1903). *Memoirs of my Nervous Illness.* (Trans.). I. Macalpine, & R.A. Hunter. R. Dinnage, (Ed.), New York: New York Review of Books, 2000.

Thomas, K. (1991). *Religion and the Decline of Magic.* London: Penguin.

Tolkien, J. R. R. (1954). *The Lord of the Rings.* London: HarperCollins, 1995.

US Surgeon General Office. (1999). *Mental Health: A Report of the Surgeon General.*

Van Gennep, A. (1908). *The Rites of Passage.* (Trans.). M. Vizedom and G. Caffee, Chicago: University of Chicago Press, 1960.

Verhaeghe, P. (1999). *Does the Woman Exist? From Freud's Hysteric to Lacan's Feminine.* (Trans.). M. du Ry, London: Rebus Press.

Verhaeghe, P. (1999). *Love in a Time of Loneliness.* (Trans.). P. Peters and T. Langham, London: Rebus Press.

Verhaeghe, P. (2001). *Beyond Gender: From subject to drive.* New York: Other Press.

Verhaeghe, P. (2004). *On Being Normal and Other Disorders: A Manual for Clinical Psychodiagnostics.* (Trans.). S. Jottkandt. New York: Other Press.

Walpole, H. (1764). *The Castle of Otranto: A Gothic Story.* Introduction, E. Clery, Oxford: Oxford University Press, 1998.

Welldon, E. (1988). *Mother, Madonna, Whore: The Idealisation and Denigration of Motherhood.* New York: Guilford Press.

Wells, H.G. (1898). *The War of the Worlds.* London: Penguin, 2005.

Williams, R. (1976). *Keywords: A Vocabulary of Culture and Society.* London: Fontana.

Žižek, S. (2004). *Iraq: The Borrowed Kettle.* London: Verso.

INDEX

DATE DUE

5-23-11			
GAYLORD			PRINTED IN U.S.A.